Beached Margin

Beached Margin
The role and representation of the
seaside resort in British films

Jez Conolly

Beached Margin © 2008 Jez Conolly

All rights reserved

No part of this publication can be reproduced, reprinted or transmitted in any form or by any means electronic or mechanical, including photocopying, recording or any other storage and retrieval system, without express written permission of the author. Permissions may be obtained via email request at: jezconolly@hotmail.com

ISBN: 978-0-9556945-0-9

For Caroline

Contents

Acknowledgements	ix
Preface	xi
Introduction: Wish you were here?	1
Chapter one: Vulgarity, morality and ritual	5
Chapter two: Haven and hell	25
Chapter three: End of the pier show?	43
Conclusion: "Somewhere spoilt"	53
Bibliography	57
Filmography	61
Index of people, places and films	65

Acknowledgements

I would like to thank Pat Poynton for her concise, timely and knowledge suggestions throughout the preparation and completion of this book.

Thanks must go to my father for letting me see lots of films for free when I was growing up, and to my brother John for his creative influence and for being the face of Cleethorpes when Andrew Kötting came knocking.

I would also like to thank fellow Meggie Jez Butler. Jez is someone I can trust to understand the cultural relevance of such terms as 'Crompton's Cakewalk' and, like me, continues to have nightmares involving the rotating clown's heads at Wonderland (never the same since it became a Sunday Market).

I would especially like to thank my lovely wife Caroline, who has put up with me rambling on about all things seasidey for the past umpteen months. Fortunately we both still love going to the seaside although we might avoid Margate.

Preface

I chose the subject for this book as a result of spending the first twenty years of my life experiencing the cultural conflux of seaside and cinema at first hand. My father, a cinema manager both before and after the Second World War, served in the RAF and afterwards settled in the English East Coast resort of Cleethorpes, that perennial butt of music hall jokes, managing the ABC Ritz and Regal cinemas.

I therefore witnessed part of the post-war parallel, although not entirely related, decline at national level of both resort and cinema as pleasure-seekers' destinations. In my youth I approached these two cultural spaces from the unusual position of conflated residential and experiential familiarity; living in a resort is *not* the same as visiting a resort, similarly enjoying privileged access behind the scenes at the cinema plus never having to pay to see a film is *not* the same as being a typical paying cinemagoer.

I would argue that my early immersion in the cinema experience and consequent appreciation and homespun understanding of film prompted me to recognise the aesthetic qualities of my seaside surroundings in a way that an upbringing bereft of such opportunities for artistic exploration would not have afforded. Since leaving the seaside environment I have wanted to explore and analyse aspects of the coastal resort experience with a formal academic perspective and through a suitable artistic or cultural medium. My choice of subject for this work has therefore not been a difficult one.

Introduction: Wish you were here?

> What a day that was – the saffron beach, with its pink and blue pails and wooden spades, its coloured tents and umbrellas, and sailing boats hurtling gaily over laughing little waves, and up on the beach other boats resting idly on their sides, smelling of seaweed and tar – the memory of it still lingers with enchantment.
>
> (Reminiscence of a boyhood visit to Southend-on-Sea.)
>
> Charles Chaplin: *My Autobiography*. London : Bodley Head, 1964

This book will investigate the exploitation of the British seaside holiday resort as a setting for film productions, examining the reasons why this environment has appealed to filmmakers and what particular qualities and characteristics specific to seaside spaces and those that inhabit them lend themselves to cinema.

The first chapter will contain some perspective on the cinematic possibilities of the seaside environment based on leading socio-cultural studies. This will involve examination of the liminal nature of resorts, as places on the margin, unterritorialised spaces that provide opportunities for socio-cultural exchanges to be observed and for dramatic situations to occur. It will look at the collision of the social classes as played out in resorts and the potential for dramatic spectacle that this presents, particularly in regard to the spectacle of the seaside family holiday.

The second chapter will focus on the position of the seaside resort as a metaphysical and dramatic threshold, the thin, shifting space between solid and liquid states, a boundary to be challenged and a barrier to be confronted, a space peopled variously by those drawn to or born of the cultural milieu, those seeking to escape or with something to hide, and those marginalized or driven to the outer edges of the land by society.

The third chapter will consider the cinematic depiction of the seaside resort and those who continue to populate it as the epitome of post-imperial faded grandeur; anachronistic, nostalgic and unfashionable. It will also look at the seaside's continuing capacity to reinvent itself and its ability to capture quintessential national idiosyncrasies, as reflected by a selection of recent film texts.

Before commencing it is worth providing a brief tonal assemblage of the broad themes explored in the whole work with some added historical context that will lead into the main discussion.

On the 1st of May 1908 George Arthur Smith, associate of the Brighton School of Filmmakers, screened an eight minute film demonstrating the new Kinemacolor two-colour process for the gathered members of the trade press. The film was entitled *A Visit to the Seaside* and briefly depicted the activities of a typical Edwardian middle class family outing to Brighton. It is historically regarded as the World's first publicly presented colour film.

That Smith should choose these familiar seaside environs as the setting for his ground-breaking film is unsurprising, not simply because of their convenient close proximity to his studio but also because of the stimulating and characteristic spectrum of colours that they offered. The setting provided Smith with a vibrant visual palette, one born of both nature and grand artifice, an invigorating schema that had inspired artists and writers since the birth of the English seaside resort.

Many aspects of the Nineteenth and early Twentieth Century seaside experience involved the consumption of either man-made images or natural vistas presented through man-made devices, from 'What the Butler Saw' vending machines on the pier to coin-operated telescopes on the promenade through to such attractions as Victorian Margate's camera obscura. Again in 1908 Britain's first purpose-built electric picture house, the Gem, was opened on the sea front at Great Yarmouth. As resorts came to cater for the inter-war mass tourism evermore ornate picture houses were erected to provide a popular wet weather activity for holidaymakers eager for mass visual stimulation.

The visual appeal of the seaside would extend to the early photographers of the Nineteenth Century and the filmmakers, pre- and post-Smith, of the twentieth century. As soon as cine cameras became available and affordable, holidaymakers would be compelled to record their own seaside sojourns for posterity, as a trawl through most any local amateur film archive will confirm.

There is a characteristically overstated chromatic key at the seaside, present in the vibrant illuminations, the brightly coloured costumes and confectionery and the sunlit golden beaches of typical twentieth century resort advertisements. This was born out famously in the exaggerated colours and figures of Donald McGill's seaside postcard illustrations and picked up in a series of paintings in the 1930s by the British Surrealist artist Edward Wadsworth, most notably in his canvas *The Beached Margin* (1937). This spectral radiance works in tandem with the succession of fabricated experiences synonymous with the seaside to produce an example of reality by proxy, what Jean Baudrillard would much later come to define as the *hyper-real* (Baudrillard 1994). Heavily mediated spaces, such as lidos, crazy golf courses, aquaria and waxwork museums, would come to be strongly associated with the seaside and provide the kind of secure, defined spaces in which people would seek to remove themselves spiritually from their comparatively muted existence.

The potential for dramatic storytelling in this realm of hyper-reality, in the name of entertainment or social commentary, has regularly drawn filmmakers to resorts in the decades since the development of commercial cinema, making it an especially important cinematic environment and one worthy of study.

Chapter one: Vulgarity, morality and ritual

> The greatest advantage in this tour was that a country tended to seep to its coast; it was concentrated there, deposited against its beaches like the tide-wrack from the sea.
>
> Paul Theroux: *Kingdom by the sea: a journey around the coast of Great Britain.* Harmondsworth : Penguin, 1984

The opening chapter will examine those factors that have drawn filmmakers to use the seaside resort as a setting for their work and will focus on the development of the British family seaside holiday experience as depicted in a selection of film texts.

These texts, spanning a period from before the Second World War up to the recent past, reflect the process of change and transgression broadly associated with British society in general over the same period, but do so courtesy of the emphasized presentation of social relationships that the seaside holiday experience engenders. Thus they provide a concentrated view of behavioural idiosyncrasies drawn together and allowed to interact and flourish by the situation and environment, a view perhaps not so readily offered by other more everyday locations, activities and situations, and therefore all the more suitable for those film practitioners looking to encapsulate aspects of the National Character or pass commentary on the state of the nation.

In them at times we can see both cross-section and the crossing of lines; we can see pre war 'mustn't grumble' meeting post war 'kiss me quick', collisions of class and culture, excess and austerity, the loosening of morals versus the buttoning up of overcoats, the convergence of holiday-makers packed into resorts resulting in complete strangers brought into close proximity, their personal space and privacy compromised. We also see the dissolution of families, the coalescence of youth and sexual awakening and how this is played out in a seaside setting, notably with regard to the promenade and beach acting variously as stage, catwalk and battleground.

Initial research of work in the wider spheres of sociology and cultural theory presents two key concepts that help to explain the dramatic appeal of the seaside to filmmakers. The first is that of the 'Carnivalesque'. This is an idea that originated in the work of the Russian theorist Mikhail Bakhtin. Bakhtin's theories are developed in *Rabelais and his world*, a text that examines the medieval origins of the carnival as a space in which conventional hierarchies of authority may be overturned. Bakhtin states that 'carnival celebrated temporary liberation from the prevailing truth and from the established order' involving a 'temporary suspension of all hierarchic distinctions and barriers' (Bakhtin 1968: 10). A brief study of the historical development of seaside resorts shows clearly that during the Nineteenth Century many elements of the Carnivalesque, previously synonymous with fairs and fetes, were pushed to the coastal periphery resulting in the gradual foundation of the resort culture that is now commonly conceived. In one of many works on the subject, John Walton suggests that the early seaside resort was 'a potential site of carnival', inaugurating 'an ephemeral regime of festive excess' (Walton 2001: 176)

Rob Shields, in his text *Places on the margin: alternative geographies of modernity*, also picks up on this theme, suggesting that such festivities were effectively banished to peripheral arenas such as the beach. It is in this work that Shields promotes the idea of 'liminality' in respect of resorts – the second key concept. Shields' suggestion is that seaside resorts function as liminal spaces because they blur the demarcation between the land and the sea, located, literally, at the margins of the nation; they possess what Shields refers to as the 'unterritorialised status of the beach, unincorporated into the system of controlled, civilised spaces' (Shields 1991: 84).

To take a step back, the term 'liminal' has been closely associated with the work of the ethnographer Victor Turner, in particular his work entitled *The ritual process*. In defining the concept of cultural and societal rites of passage Turner refers to three phases of transition; separation, margin and aggregation (Turner 1969). The Latin term for margin is *limen* signifying 'boundary' or 'threshold', hence the term 'liminal' which can be used to describe those ambiguous, unclassifiable, transitory spaces or zones through which individuals may pass and in which social conventions are loosened thereby allowing for more permissive and playful behaviour.

Shields regards seaside resorts, in particular tourist beaches, as examples of such liminal zones, not simply because of the physical marginal space they occupy between land and sea, but also because they link in to the mythic notion of an intersectional environment between points of arrival and departure in which preconceived rules and codes do not apply, leading to danger, excitement and a multitude of possibilities. They are what Kate Fox describes as 'social micro-climates' affording 'cultural remission' away from normal social controls and allowing heightened levels of familiarity, the need for which is ordinarily masked by a collective tendency to conform to the accepted norm in commonplace situations (Fox 2004: 89).

The concept of liminality is not limited to geographical spaces. Turner's work discusses those periods in a person's life experience that constitute a transition, a prime example being the adolescent phase between childhood and adulthood. Turner notes that it is common within social groups for such phases to be associated with ritualistic patterns of behaviour, or initiation, demonstrably marking the transition. This initiative behaviour is in turn frequently associated with particular locations or sites that are apart from the normal environment. These sites by their very nature lend themselves to this process of change, therefore in recent decades it is unsurprising that seaside resort spaces have become associated with initial teenage explorations of sexuality and promiscuity. Interestingly Turner also regards these liminal phases as often also being associated with periods of temporary seclusion or isolation, a point that will be discussed in the second chapter in relation to characters in films seeking escape or concealment at the seaside.

The creative appeal of beach and resort spaces to artists, writers and filmmakers can be summed up by this quote from Jean-Didier Urbain's *Sur la plage*: 'The beach is a spectacle. It is a theatre where society unveils and strips itself bare… the beach is nobody's native soil. It is a tablet unwritten on, an abstraction, an empty and rootless place' (Urbain 1994: 19).

In providing what amounts to a blank canvas accompanied by a vibrant palette of possibilities, together with its positioning as a pan-societal socio-cultural parade route, the seaside resort offers a singular lens through which to scrutinise the extraordinary dramas of everyday life.

By way of contextualising the film texts discussed in this and subsequent chapters it is worth outlining the historical development of the seaside family holiday over the period that they cover. The Twentieth Century saw the ritual of the summer holiday, once the preserve of the wealthy few, extend to encompass the breadth of the social substrate. The seaside holiday in particular would grow to become the perfect metaphor of the consumer moment, a time/place tailored for the modern industrial society to experience a modern transcendence akin to traditional religious and seasonal rituals. People on holiday sought freedom from ordinary, regulated, mechanical time and an opportunity to enjoy the freedom to spend beyond their ordinary budgetary limits, even if they could ill afford it. Year-round saving and austerity in preparation for the holiday was widespread, as it meant that the ordinariness of everyday life was relieved in the annual period of luxury. Crucially, holiday consumption fulfilled a need for both autonomy and sociability, allowing for the empowerment of the one among the many.

In the inter-war years the popularity of seaside resorts situated relatively close to the main industrial areas grew rapidly as gradually more of the lower-middle and working class population were able to afford to go on holiday, albeit very often on a modest budget. This developed as more employers began to grant paid holiday time for their employees. In the decades before, primarily among the huge cotton manufacturing workforce in North West England, the only holiday-making opportunities for many families came during 'Wakes Week', usually in July or August, when mill owners would allow their workers a brief (unpaid) respite to allow time for mill machinery maintenance.

In 1938 the Holidays With Pay Act reached the statute book resulting in a major upturn in resort visitor numbers. According to Walton the number of employees earning up to £250 a year with paid holiday entitlement leapt from 3 million in March 1938 to 11 million by June 1939 (Walton 2000: 57). Seaside resorts therefore increasingly served as social melting pots in the first decades of the Twentieth Century, bringing together families from across the class spectrum and provoking social interactions outside typical daily life. A greater number of young adults from working class backgrounds, particularly women, were better able to experience the relative freedom offered by resorts.

The popularity of seaside resorts allowed local councils and private enterprise to invest in new attractions; piers, hotels and cinemas were built or modernized, and newly-constructed lidos added another locus for gregarious pleasure-seeking. Lidos particularly, with their open air swimming pools, provided a safe, mediated display space for those intent on the flesh-exposing practice of sunbathing, itself something of a new national phenomenon in the 1930s. Billy Butlin opened his first holiday camp in Skegness in 1936, offering a week's holiday for a week's pay and accommodating up to 5,500 holidaymakers, thereby changing the face of family holiday-making for decades.

The 1920s and 1930s also saw resorts play host to instances of popular vulgar spectacle, descendants of the Victorian freak shows and peep shows. In the latter decade such lurid attractions often revolved around starvation or endurance, a prime example being Harold Davidson, the defrocked ex-Rector of Stiffkey, who caused a national scandal by facing trial for allegedly fraternizing with prostitutes in his parish. Davidson appeared on Blackpool's Golden Mile in 1932 encased in a barrel (then again in a glass case in 1935) and fasted for 14 days supposedly as a protest against his prosecution. On the first day of the fast 10,000 people paid twopence each to squint at Davidson apparently starving to death inside the barrel (Braggs and Harris 2000).

A valuable and defining antecedent to the discussion is Arthur Houghton's once-controversial play *Hindle Wakes*. Houghton's work, now largely overlooked, was often marked by the influence of Henrik Ibsen, with *Hindle Wakes* frequently likened to *A Doll's House* in its thematic focus on freedom from the bondage of social and gendered duty. Houghton shared Ibsen's empathy for women and abhorrence of patriarchal domination. First staged in 1912 and subsequently filmed four times for cinema and twice for television, *Hindle Wakes* is set over the course of a Wakes Week holiday spent partly in Blackpool, and tells of a young, respectable, unmarried working class woman allowing herself a few days of casual relations with the single son of an affluent family.

That a young female character should regard a brief fling with a well-off young man in exactly the same way that *he* might see it - as a transient 'bit of fun' that in no way obliged her to marry him – was daring for its time. Furthermore, for the central character to walk away from her disapproving parents, who believe that the couple should marry for the sake of appearances, in order to make a life free from patriarchal influence, verged on the revolutionary. It is also an example of a significant transgression of the established order facilitated by the Carnivalesque experienced during time spent in Blackpool's liminal climes.

Arguably the finest filmed version of the play is Maurice Elvey's 1927 silent production. Elvey, who had filmed the play previously in 1918, revisited the story in light of the evolution of montage and cinematography driven by D.W. Griffith, Sergei Eisenstein and German Expressionism, and used the opportunity to heighten the play's examination of class and sexual self-determination. Although the second half of the film lapses into staged melodrama the first two or three reels demonstrate a skillful use of location filming to give in turn a documentary feel to the cotton mill and an hallucinatory quality to the resort.

An early intertitle clearly signals the film's themes of release from the routine of work, and from the social controls of family, community and workplace: 'For one short week in each long year the mills of Lancashire are silent and the bond slaves of Cotton know the ecstasy of freedom.' Images of characters' shoes are used to convey social standing (at that time it was a common practice to determine a person's class by the quality and condition of their footwear), for example the mill workers leave behind a litter of discarded shoes when they hurry off to begin their holiday, literally kicking off their mundane roles and leaving them behind on the factory floor.

The key sequence in Elvey's film, a seven minute unbroken montage coming twenty minutes into the film, is a phantasmagoric distillation of Blackpool's permissive ingredients. Having portrayed the workers enslaved by the machinery of the mill Elvey then shows them liberated by the same modern mechanical technology, now placed in the service of their entertainment. It is present in the roller coaster rides, the searchlights that pore over the hundreds of foxtrotting couples in the Tower Ballroom and the ubiquitous Illuminations transforming the resort into a glittering dreamland and probing the darkened, sexualized nightlife.

The early mill scenes possess a documentary immediacy that contrasts with the dizzying camerawork in the Blackpool sequence. Elvey mounted cameras on rotating ferris wheels and speeding rollercoaster cars, including an uncut shot of the entire rollercoaster ride from a passenger's point of view, all to give the 'world' of Blackpool a breathless, kinetic sweep. Viewed from high above in a single lingering take, the dancers in the ballroom seem to swarm in waves across the dancefloor, showing that the people are an integral component in the heady, pulsating atmosphere.

This is a near-orgiastic, unleashed festival of emancipation, but importantly the collective pursuit of the people at Blackpool is shown to empower the individual, in this case the lead female character, to seek independence upon her return home. In his work on tourism theory *The Tourist Gaze*, John Urry drew a distinction between what he described as the 'romantic gaze' among tourists, one possessing 'emphasis upon solitude, privacy and a personal, semi-spiritual relationship with the object of the gaze', and the 'collective gaze', which 'necessitates the presence of large numbers of other people [who] give atmosphere or a sense of carnival to a place. They indicate that this is *the* place to be and that one should not be elsewhere' (Urry 2001: 43). The Blackpool experienced in *Hindle Wakes* is the epitome of the object of the convivial collective gaze.

Implicit in Urry's theory is that the romantic gaze is a predominantly middle class concept while the collective gaze is characteristically, although not exclusively, a proletarian phenomenon. Interestingly in Nineteenth Century Blackpool crowds were geographically segregated along class lines controlled by Blackpool Corporation through restrictive bye-laws and distinctions drawn in popular guidebooks. Certain areas were recognised as the preserve of middle class visitors, most notably the North Pier, while the South Pier (later to become known as the Central Pier and popularly referred to as the 'Peoples' Pier') catered for the working class (Webb 2005). This segregation would begin to dissolve with the coming of mass tourism in the Twentieth Century. It can be argued that this form of sociable, collective holidaymaking provided a means of making sense of life for many people through intercourse with other people outside of their normal experience, a process through which identity and belonging was and still is socially constructed (Shotter 1993). The seaside holiday therefore offers an important social arena for refiguring identities, a theme that is repeatedly picked up in the film texts that feature in this chapter.

Two examples of pre and post war seaside-set features worthy of analysis and comparison are Carol Reed's *Bank Holiday* (1938) and Ken Annakin's *Holiday Camp* (1947). Both offer a kaleidoscope view of the British public seeking pleasure at a bustling resort, deliberately making use of the 'melting pot' communality engendered by the environment to portray a contemporary social microcosm.

The central plot of Reed's *Bank Holiday*, superficially a sentimental tale of love, loss and separation, is liberally decorated with a host of episodic, often ironic, gently mocking vignettes and side-stories featuring contrasting 'ordinary' working class characters. These serve to illustrate patterns of social interaction associated with the rapid passage of workforce tourists through a typical pre-war resort. The film is clearly influenced by the type of documentary realism that had emerged in Britain in the early 1930s. Reed himself would go on to direct wartime documentaries commissioned by the Army Kinematograph Service. It contains a number of quickly-cut atmospheric fly-on-the-wall long shots and crane shots of hundreds of holidaymakers shown leaving their domestic 'ant-colony' London setting, disembarking at their destination, going about the business of pleasure-seeking and battling the vagaries of a wet August Bank Holiday weekend in Brighton.

This documentarist depiction of a slice of mass society at play was partly designed to capture what by 1938 people across the class spectrum had come to regard as a marker for citizenship, almost a national right to pleasure that many more people than had previously been the case could expect to exercise. It was also partly intended to present a unified collective 'brave face' to the film's audience at a time of impending war. Indeed the billboards and newspaper headlines that flit across the screen expressly communicate this, giving the sense that this is the moment to make hay while the sun shines, irrespective of class or financial standing. This unification is cemented towards the end of the film when the miscellany of characters come together at 'the Grand', the resort's principal hotel, in an enactment of the dissolution of class divides permitted by the locale and the occasion.

Despite this social agglomeration, Reed took pains to paint in idiosyncratic character details so as to draw cultural distinctions between characters, all done in the name of satire, and for that matter added realism. That said, although the procession of supporting characters encountered at the resort serve simply as soft targets for Reed's mockery, and therefore lack any great depth, the satire that he employed in depicting them is not borne out of a patronising cynicism, it is more the work of an eavesdropper seeking to observe his subject with a sympathetic eye in order to present an affectionate picture of society, a view bereft of class prejudice and thereby a film able to appeal to a wide range of cinema-going audiences, no doubt an important factor in its not-inconsiderable commercial success.

This is not to suggest that the film should be wholly defined as a cosy, charming experience. It possesses a sexual frankness somewhat ahead of its time whilst echoing the female emancipation theme of *Hindle Wakes*. The plot opens with a nurse's sudden infatuation for the husband of a woman she had been nursing who has died in childbirth that very day, a situation that the nurse finds rather upsetting considering she was about to embark on her first dirty weekend at the seaside with her boyfriend! This frankness is further revealed in scenes involving competitors in a beauty contest. One contestant, 'Miss Mayfair', not only sets out to seduce the senior judge but also parades along the pier with another man minus her underwear, a fact revealed as she walks over the slatted floor of the pier by a jealous opponent who happens to be sitting below. Most tellingly, there is little doubt in the shots of crowds of trippers that, unable to find or afford rooms for the night, many among them intend to indulge in nocturnal sexual encounters on the beach. Indeed these shots of ordinary working class people dreaming and musing over their aspirations as they contemplate a night spent by the sea capture the essence of how the liminal seaside space facilitates thoughts and deeds of unencumbered and radically celebratory possibilities.

Peter William Evans, in his recent study of Reed's career, chooses to focus on the central characters in *Bank Holiday*, usually overshadowed in critiques of the film by the parade of supporting players, and finds some interesting attributes in their behaviour and motivation with regard to both sexual morality and social class. In particular the character of the nurse, played by Margaret Lockwood in her first substantial role, displays a marked indifference towards the moral and social conventions of the time. Her willingness to spend the Bank Holiday weekend with a man to whom she is not married, together with her romantic fantasy about another man she has only just met and who is from a higher class, represent a significant transgression and moral ambiguity. Evans describes the character as possessing 'a blend of submissiveness and emancipation, her obliging nature no guarantee of conformity' (Evans 2005: 12).

As such she presented 1938 audiences with a dilemma; should they admire her initiative and self-determination in seeking to move beyond her social and gendered constraints by pursuing a romance with the middle class widower or should they judge her negatively for even entertaining such thoughts? Reed includes a shot of Lockwood on an escalator at a London Underground station, at the beginning of her journey to the seaside, with a film poster in view declaring '*Sinners*: love was their only crime', further signifying the ambiguity of the character's motivation.

It is interesting to note that Lockwood's character returns to her role as nurse at the end of the film, when we see her attending the bedside of the middle-class widower following his failed suicide attempt. When she declares 'Everybody comes back. The holiday is over' she is effectively acknowledging that the transgressive feelings that she felt permitted to experience during her time at the resort must be reined in now that those involved are relocated back to their normal surroundings and situations, with social roles and distances reinstated. This illustrates how the resort allowed for, and probably provoked, a relaxation of the rules of relationships.

Ken Annakin's debut feature, the post-war *Holiday Camp* shares a number of aspects with the pre-war *Bank Holiday* but the years that separate the films provoke several departures in tone, content and commentary. Annakin effectively served an apprenticeship under Carol Reed during the war years, Reed having spotted his potential while working on the recruitment film *We Serve* (1942), and Annakin would later acknowledge *Bank Holiday* as the model for *Holiday Camp*, his first attempt at a feature length production (Hare 2003). His wartime documentary-making experience shows in his extensive use of location shooting at Butlins in Filey for *Holiday Camp*. The opening shots in particular, of the arrival of holidaymakers at the train station, their ferrying to the camp in a fleet of coaches and the arduous process of locating their assigned chalets are as much an historical record as similar scenes in the earlier *Sing As We Go* (Basil Dean 1934), a film perhaps more often lauded as a document of its time. Like *Bank Holiday*, the film aims to present a cross-section of the pleasure-seeking English, but notably the range of characters on display are picked from across the social spectrum. In a film that introduced the Huggetts, the archetypal salt-of-the-earth working class family who would go on to feature centrally in a series of films, we also encounter individuals from further up the class system, such as Dennis Price's sinister ex-RAF Squadron Leader and Flora Robson's bereaved spinster. By showing the working class democratically rubbing shoulders with the middle and upper-middle class, both young and old, the film captures the spirit of Bakhtin's Carnivalesque concept, outlined succinctly by the theorist in another of his works: 'What is suspended [in carnival] first of all is hierarchical structure and all the forms of terror, reverence, piety, and etiquette connected with it - that is, everything resulting from sociohierarchical inequality or any other form of inequality among people (including age).' (Bakhtin 1984: 122-123)

There is a clear attempt to blur class boundaries in the name of presenting an egalitarian picture of post war Britain. Scripted by Ted Willis, whose work would come to be characterized by its left-wing tendency, the film shows people from across the class spectrum wearing similar clothes, sharing chalets, eating together in the same cafeterias and dancing the hokey cokey together in the same ballroom. There is little linguistic divide between characters either; although Joe and Ethel Huggett's dialect marks them clearly as working class their children's accents are barely distinguishable from those of the manifestly middle class characters (although this is probably more a product of drama school training at the time than any deliberate reduction of class differences)(Marriott 1997).

The fact that *Holiday Camp* was produced in the immediate post-war period at a time when structured mass communal leisure was starting to gain in popularity also helps to explain why the presence of a range of social class types at the camp is less incongruous than an audience today might assume. The Butlins camps were able to boast the likes of Anthony Eden, Lady Violet Bonham Carter and the Archbishop of York among other luminaries who could be counted among their guests. Beyond this kind of publicity the privations of the post war years certainly meant that many more people further up the class ladder were prepared to entertain the prospect of a few days in a camp than would have been the case before the war.

Holiday Camp then was very much in tune with the 1945-1951 Atlee Government's drive towards radical social inclusivity as a means of countering widespread austerity. Esmond Knight's blind camp announcer's meditation on the sounds of camp life pointedly encapsulates this post war socialistic tone: 'Do you see what I see? ... One of the strangest sights of the Twentieth Century; the great mass of people all fighting for the one thing you can't get by fighting for it – happiness.' Despite this egalitarian intent, relative poverty overwhelmingly defines the characters' response to their surroundings. Joe Huggett's attitude towards the camp's amenities and activities sums this up; when his wife baulks at an arduous group activity on the beach he reminds her to 'Stick it, mother. Good money we're paying for this. You don't want to waste it.'

Wartime associations pervade the campers' approach to their surroundings in the film. To put this into historical context, holiday camps were requisitioned during the hostilities to variously house evacuees, internees, military personnel and relocated workers. The Butlins camp at Filey where *Holiday Camp*'s location work was shot was only part-built when war broke out, but Billy Butlin negotiated a deal with the Government to complete its construction for use by the RAF. Butlin not only provided cheap mass accommodation and catering for the Forces personnel, he also won the right to buy the camp back off the Government at the end of the war, meaning that he had a new, ready-made camp at the start of peacetime just when there would be an upturn in demand for holidays. Butlin was also involved in a morale-raising capacity during the war in assisting the organisation of the 'Holidays at Home' campaign to address the leisure needs of wartime workers (Barton 2005). So *Holiday Camp*'s characters refer to the 'control tower' where the camp announcer resides, the uniformed NCO-like Redcoats steer and cajole holidaymakers into partaking of the facilities and events take place in a mass regimented fashion to strict time parameters.

Despite this regressive inclination there is much in *Holiday Camp* that projects a more progressive and morally ambiguous outlook, largely due to the setting's communal, liminal permissiveness. As passing examples we see the campers being urged to kiss strangers on the dancefloor and Joe Huggett cheating at cards, albeit as a means of teaching some unscrupulous cardsharps a lesson. More deeply though the film effectively condones sex before marriage between two supporting characters, although it is made plain that the offending couple, Michael and the pregnant Valerie, intend to get married eventually.

Five years after the release of *Holiday Camp* Lindsay Anderson shot his twelve minute montage *O Dreamland*, and in doing so presented a significantly less sympathetic snapshot of the similar subject matter. Made for just £100 and shot on 16mm in and around Margate's seafront funfair Dreamland, the film is now regarded as an important entry in the roster of Free Cinema films of the 1950s. It is also one of the most personal to come out of that movement; Anderson displays a misanthropic distaste for the English at play amid the seediness and noisy vulgarity of the funfair. This is a film that Anderson himself regarded as 'a song of experience...almost a hate film' (Anderson, Ryan 2004: 59) although any critique of it should reflect the fact that it was shot extremely quickly and spontaneously with little if any desire on Anderson's part to have it widely exhibited.

There are echoes in *O Dreamland* of the documentary footage 'ant colony' shots from *Bank Holiday* and mass entertainment activities featured in *Holiday Camp*, but instead of the hasty, high-spirited descent upon the resort we are shown in Reed's film and the breezy 'chin-up and enjoy it' attitude of Annakin's characters, we see packs of trippers, deposited by a troupe of charabancs and left to roam aimlessly around Dreamland's arcades and attractions in a state of mute disengagement. Parents and children alike appear quite miserable, almost zombie-like; they disconnectedly gaze at the horrors of the wax museum, they drink tea and consume greasy food in a vast characterless canteen with little apparent sense of enjoyment or communality. There is not much fun to be found at the fair, indeed the clear comment is that the people depicted simply do not know how to enjoy themselves. Almost nobody is seen to smile throughout the film, instead we see a cross-section of the weary, blank-faced post war masses practically herded from one corner of the funfair to the other by bingo callers, entertainment officials and stall-holders, shots frequently accompanied by an overlaid soundtrack of deeply ironic mechanical laughter sourced from the funfair's resident 'Laughing Policeman' animated puppet, or the slushy jukebox intonations of Frankie Laine's 'I Believe'.

A common critical position on *O Dreamland* suggests that Anderson reflected a middle class condescension towards the working class, picturing them alternately as being exploited, or being complicit in their exploitation. For example, there are numerous shots of the holidaymakers' feet as they shamble from one attraction to the next amid a maelstrom of litter – perhaps an echo of the workers' discarded shoes in *Hindle Wakes* – suggesting that the people are only so much flotsam adrift in a mess of their own making. While this is fair criticism it could be argued that the director's position was borne as much out of a broader sense of disappointment, frustration and protest at what he perceived as the Nation's post war social sclerosis, it's peoples' mass anonymity and apparent difficulty in shaking off its wartime 'make do' attitude and associated behavioural tropes. Although Anderson's tone is unquestionably derisive, his disenchantment is redressed by an obvious fidelity for the subject. Rather than simply make scornful representations of the working class, he in fact reveals the peoples' spiritual poverty and loss of identity and thereby their collective difficulty in finding amusement or pleasure even when it is laid out before them at the funfair. His venom is largely directed at Dreamland itself by presenting Margate and the tourist experience as shabby and superficial. As Gavin Lambert described at the time of the film's first public screening in 1956:

> "Everything is ugly... It is almost too much. The nightmare is redeemed by the point of view, which, for all the unsparing candid camerawork and the harsh, inelegant photography, is emphatically humane. Pity, sadness, even poetry is infused into this drearily tawdry, aimlessly hungry world." (Lambert 1956)

This cynical take on holidaymakers would be picked up some ten years later at a time when the traditional family holiday was beginning to fracture and the phenomenon of the empowered teenager was emerging. The rebellious youth cultures that developed in the 1950s and 1960s were inevitably drawn to the turbulent heterodoxy that the culturally ungoverned spaces of seaside resorts promised.

Michael Winner's *The System* (1964) steps inside the province of a group of young men headed by Tinker Taylor, a libidinous souvenir photographer played by Oliver Reed, who spend their summers working tourist locations by day and seducing young women by night. Unlike the previous films discussed, in *The System* we are not sharing in the collective gaze of the holidaymakers, instead we are privy to the point of view of Tinker and his colleagues as residents of the resort, complete with a hugely cynical assessment of the tourists that they prey on. At the beginning of the film Tinker educates a new member of his cabal by contemptuously referring to the tourists as 'Grockles' and defining them thus:

> The Grockle is closely related to the Troglodyte. The troglodytes lived in a natural cave, stoned their grandparents to death and came out three times a year for food. A Grockle puts his grandparents in an old folks' home, lives in a pre-cast concrete cave and comes out once a year to make a religious pilgrimage to the sea from whence he came. There he ceremoniously rolls up his trousers and dips his feet into the water.

Tinker and his cohort are not so much predatory as they are parasitic. They shamelessly live off the people who visit the resort in both a financial and cynically recreational sense. At one point Tinker reflects upon his approach to the visitors when in conversation with an associate: 'We must take what we can from the tourists, gather nuts against a hard winter'. To compound this cynical attitude Tinker's wider moral code is brought into question early on in the film when he coolly advises a friend, whose girlfriend is pregnant, to talk her into having an abortion rather than settle down as a family, even offering him the address of an abortionist.

Yet despite this initially negative depiction Tinker is gradually revealed as a complex, restless individual and ultimately a sympathetic character who employs the roguish playboy persona to mask his loss of identity. He is not only trapped in the liminality of the resort but also caught in the space between class distinctions, belonging neither to the 'Grockle' set nor the Bourgeoisie, embodied by Society Girl Nicola who captures then breaks his heart. *The System* is in part Anderson's *O Dreamland* frustrations writ large, fleshed out in the form of Tinker's 'angry young man' social exclusion and introspection. It takes the superficial social melting pot of the resort with the reliance on its rapid throughput of visitors and seasonal limitations to ensnare the character in a situation of disengagement and powerlessness leading to his crisis of identity. This crisis mirrors the wider sense of disenfranchisement being felt by youths in the late 1950s and early 1960s, a period of change that is examined in more detail in chapter three.

1964, the year of *The System*'s release, saw much publicized violence among youths at a string of seaside resorts around the Bank Holiday weekends. Sociologist Stanley Cohen coined the phrase 'moral panic' in discussing the Media and political reaction of the time to these Mods versus Rockers riots (Cohen 1972). He and others perceived these contrived instances of journalistic hysteria and indignation as serving to reassert the dominance of an established value system at a time of anxiety or crisis. This period was evoked fifteen years later in Franc Roddam's *Quadrophenia* (1979). The film presents a vivid encapsulation of the adolescent liminal experience in its story of teenage angst finding an outlet through the amphetamine-fuelled activities of a Lambretta-riding gang of Mods, most strikingly in the final act when the scooter gang descends upon Brighton. This is all about an exhilarating point of liminality, meaningful to the one but facilitated by the many. It is what Adrian Martin describes specifically in relation to *Quadrophenia* as:

> …that intense, suspended moment between yesterday and tomorrow, between childhood and adulthood, between being a nobody and a somebody, when everything is in question, and anything is possible. (Martin 1994: 64).

The central character Jimmy is the embodiment of the emergent 1960s youth culture working class hedonist, desperate for the weekend thrill and bored with the weekday job that finances that thrill. The seaside resort is where his identity is refigured, it is where he is taken outside of his class role and away from his uncomprehending family to become the one thing that he wants to be: different. Brighton presents him with the opportunity to forge an identity and it is in the Brighton liminality that all aspects of his character come closest to integration. A line from the Pete Townshend-penned soundtrack song *Bell Boy* captures this aspiration:

> The beach is a place where a man can feel
>
> He's the only soul in the world that's real

Ironically Jimmy finds 'difference' through the strict Mod sub-cultural dress code and status symbols of the sharp suit, the parka, the pills and the scooter, but it is this uniformity that provides him with a social and symbolic context in which he can become a part of a collective identity and thereby develop his individual self-esteem. The Brighton riot is the act that makes his ambition a reality, albeit temporarily. It is in this moment that he becomes a 'face', on an even footing with his associates, able to rub shoulders with those among his clique he most aspires to be like, most notably alongside his idol Ace Face, in Jimmy's eyes the ultimate expression of Mod culture. He is also ready to consummate his relationship with girlfriend Steph in a bout of hectic perpendicular sex stolen down a back alley during a hiatus in the mid-riot chase sequence. But this being a frenetic, momentary state born of the passage through Brighton's permissive threshold, it rapidly becomes apparent that the euphoric payoff of the experience is unsustainable. Indeed the consequences prove catastrophic. Jimmy loses everything; Steph to his best friend, his best friend (over Steph), his job, his family, his scooter and, most dramatically, the respect he had developed for his hero Ace Face. By riding off the edge of the cliffs on Ace Face's scooter at the end of the film the dream that Jimmy got to live on the tumultuous beaches of Brighton now dies on the deserted reaches at Dover.

Perhaps what we witness in Tinker's failure to break out of his trap-within-a-trap in *The System* and Jimmy's disillusionment with Mod culture and the impermanence of his Brighton experience in *Quadrophenia* begins to support a counter-reading of Bakhtin's theory of the Carnivalesque particularly when applied to the activities of post war youth cultures. Rather than facilitating freedom for frustrated adolescence it could be argued that the liminal seaside carnival experience is an example of an activity that works to *contain* as much as to release youthful energies. It could be viewed as a time/place that is specifically designed to allow a limited expression of independence and liberty within designated, mediated and constrained spaces, one that permits monitored and metered behavioural transgressions which can be readily commercially exploited (Mallan & Pearce 2003).

Whilst it is possible to regard resorts as representative of a different kind of liminal zone, between pleasure and commodification, populated by contained visitants led by market forces to buy into an illusion of unrestricted hedonism, it can be stated that any such controlled and limited 'masquerade' is largely understood and accepted by its participants for what it is. In other words, despite the semi-enforced herding of holidaymakers cynically depicted in O *Dreamland*, most post war trippers are happy and willing to regard the petty restrictions of a resort holiday as a preferable, orchestrated, temporary release from the more pressing dominant confinements of their day-to-day existence. Moreover, despite the best efforts of the forces of commerce, resort liminality cannot be wholly sequestered and restructured for profit. It remains possible for more subtle transgressions and subsequent refigured identities and evolutions to take place within the 'order' of the 'chaos'.

A relatively recent example of a film that shows its characters drawing upon the liminal opportunities provided by a resort in order to evolve is Gurinder Chadha's *Bhaji On The Beach* (1993). The film depicts a day-trip by a group of Asian women to the resort of Blackpool and follows the characters through their various journeys of self-discovery and examination of their personal and collective values. The director's choice of Blackpool as the setting for *Bhaji On The Beach* is apposite. The lurid, semi-hallucinogenic quality of its attractions together with its iconic status as a very British working class leisure Mecca allows Chadha to portray the situations and interactions that she sought in order to explore themes of displacement, racial/cultural hybridity, and challenges to contemporary British Asian gender roles.

The resort's carnivalesque qualities and locations are used to illustrate a cultural fusion taking place. The women's minibus journey from Birmingham to Blackpool is accompanied by a Punjabi version of the Cliff Richard song *Summer Holiday*. Upon encountering the illuminations on the Golden Mile one character declares 'Bombay!' and sees parallels to the Hindu festivities of Diwali. Another imagines being pursued by a suitor across the Winter Gardens in a style reminiscent of a Bollywood film. The younger Asian characters indulge in many of the traditional activities associated with the seaside, from candy floss and amusement arcades to alcohol consumption and fleeting holiday romances. Even the older members of the party, initially resistant to compromising their cultural values, allow this other tradition into their experience, albeit with a sprinkle of curry powder on their soggy chips.

Blackpool's history is such that it is seen to embody the freedom of the working man or woman from bourgeois constraints. It is today characterised as 'the playground of the North' in tourist literature. Auberon Waugh summed it up thus: 'It is the big rock candy coated mountain of proletarian aspirations' (Waugh 1979). Tony Bennett observes that Blackpool has historically constructed itself as an imperial space 'at the centre of the nation and, even more grandiosely, of the Empire' (Bennett 1986: 147). Traces of this construction, such as the South Pier's 'Indian' façade and the Pleasure Beach's 'Maharajah's Palace' entrance serve to 'inveigle the pleasure-seeker in relations of complicity with imperialist values and sentiments' (ibid: 141). By placing her characters in this archetypal white imperialist landscape and indulging in archetypal white cultural activities – huddling in deckchairs on the beach, paddling in the tide, taking in the view from the top of Blackpool Tower – Chadha disrupts the pervasive Britishness that the resort represents by paradoxically showing them able to comfortably assimilate the cultural challenges that they encounter without compromising their own culture.

In every sense the seaside setting in *Bhaji On The Beach* conforms to Urbain's 'tablet unwritten on' definition; despite its historic cultural connotations the resort permits all-comers liberation through exposure to play and excess. The Asian women all experience a personal freedom of sorts but as a group they are released to acquire a sense of Britishness denied them by dominant discourses and representations of race. This is truly the beach and seaside environment working as a transformative liminal space, a non-conforming place that allows for tensions to be exposed, true feelings to be expressed and boundaries between race, age and gender to be dissolved.

In order to resolve the characters' respective situations, for them to be transformed, it seems they must travel to and pass through the liminal space provided by Blackpool, but the permanence of any such change is left open to question. What remains unanswered at the end of the film is just how much of the transformation will prevail once they return to Birmingham. Simi, the most political member of the group urges her companions to take the opportunity provided by the day trip to free themselves from what she describes as the 'patriarchal demands' made upon them and throw off 'the double yoke of sexism and racism'. The suggestion is that this forging of a new collective identity is transient and can only be sustained in the escapist environment provided by the resort, something of an echo of Margaret Lockwood's 'Everyone comes back, the holiday is over' sentiment at the end of *Bank Holiday*. However the final scenes shot amongst the breakwaters underneath the resort's Central Pier illustrate that at least some of the women have permanently torn down the barriers that have previously contained them. When the matriarchal Asha rushes to the aid of the younger Ginder, who is facing a physical attack from her husband, she has made the journey from critic to defender of the values of the younger generation of Asian females and there is no reason to believe that this is a temporary relaxation of her position.

Ginder's husband's attack highlights an additional interesting element of the Carnivalesque. There are warnings implicit in Victor Turner's work that the historically marginalized position of women in general society has often placed them in particular danger during times of carnival, the point being that the temporary consensual suspension of accepted laws of behaviour in the liminal time/place of the holiday can be misinterpreted, leaving women and other marginalized individuals vulnerable and open to abuse (Isaak 1996). The group of women in *Bhaji On The Beach* have an early taste of this when they encounter a vanload of men at a motorway service station who recognize that the women are in carnival mode and make what they regard as acceptable vociferous mock sexual advances. What is proffered as a sexual invitation is really an exertion of attempted control over the females who are viewed as having slipped outside of the laws of control as perceived by the group of males. When the women assert their position of social respectability they receive insults. The themes of marginalization, alienation, containment and exploitation in a seaside resort setting will be explored further in the next chapter.

Chapter two: Haven and hell

> Margate is beautiful, romantic, charismatic, sad, eccentric and screwed-up... You don't lose your virginity there, you have it broken into.
>
> Tracey Emin
>
> Quoted in: Steve Boggan: Wish you were here? Margate prepares for its rites of passage, Tracey. *The Independent (London)* July 28, 2001

Having chronologically plotted the course of the pre and post war holiday experience through a number of film texts in the first chapter, this next chapter will look more closely at several other distinct but interrelated elements that explain why people are to be found in a seaside setting and how and why these elements have been captured on film.

It will initially examine themes of displacement, exile and 'otherness'. Aside from the passage of holidaymakers, resorts have come to play host to those marginalized from society because of their association with a subjugated cultural, racial or sexual minority, or simply vulnerable, alienated individuals either driven to or deposited at the outer edges of the land or consciously seeking escape or a place to hide. In this context the carnivalesque seaside spaces discussed in the first chapter take on a darker aspect, allowing filmmakers the chance to capture that which lies beneath the grand artifice and tempered grotesquery of resorts, and by extension the country: a seaside of seediness, exploitation and corruption populated by gangsters, petty criminals, unscrupulous businesses, delinquents and murderers only too eager to prey upon the weak and disenfranchised. In probing the metaphysical and dramatic threshold represented by coastal spaces, filmmakers have been able to capture the decisive, liberating moments of passage through the brink that separates characters from a state of constraint to a position of relative emancipation.

As discussed in the previous chapter, Gurinder Chadha's *Bhaji On The Beach* drew on the Asian community's experiences of diaspora, the process of cultural and geographic displacement, and by placing the drama in Blackpool the director was able to utilize the resort as a socio-cultural crossing point through which her characters could encounter a concentrated form of Britishness, question their own sense of identity within this setting and explore the socio-cultural hybridity going on around them. Chadha lightheartedly emphasizes this hybridization by bringing her Asian characters into contact with white members of the Blackpool community in various theatrical or hyperreal alternative guises – the burger-flipping 'Cowboys', the 'Arab' commentator with a North-West accent at the Arabian Derby camel race attraction, the shark-costumed performers of 'Moby Dick On Ice', the turban-wearing snake charmer on the pier – all to wryly illustrate a process of crude cultural synthesis. By the end of the film the characters have an enhanced sense of identity, community and belonging.

Pawel Pawlikowski's *Last Resort* (2000) presents a very different reception of 'outsiders' by the sea. It is an inversion of the reasons why people might otherwise be drawn to this kind of liminal space; on the one hand it features characters who desperately wish to be elsewhere but are penned in and detained pending a bureaucratic decision, on the other it portrays somebody who lacks the will to leave and instead seeks solace in its confines. The film tells the story of Tanya, a young Russian woman, and her ten-year-old son Artiom, who arrive in England hoping to meet the man Tanya considers to be her fiancé. The fiancé fails to appear, and threatened with being sent back to Russia, Tanya impulsively claims political asylum. Mother and son are rapidly deposited in the fictional rundown South East coast 'resort' of Stonehaven (doubling for Margate where the film was shot) to await the results of the processing of her asylum claim. Tanya and Artiom find themselves housed in a dismal high rise flat overlooking the bedraggled Dreamland funfair, the same Dreamland to feature in Lindsay Anderson's 1950s short film, now seen to be completely run down. Tanya befriends Alfie, an amusement arcade manager and bingo caller, who does his best to make her bleak life more palatable by giving their soulless flat a coat of paint, providing a television and introducing them to Indian food. Conflict arises when Tanya turns to internet pornography in an attempt to raise the cash to return to Russia. However with Alfie's help Tanya and Artiom eventually make good their escape.

Last Resort positions its drama at the heart of the post Balkans conflict 'moral panic' surrounding the accommodation of immigrants from Eastern Europe and is the starting point for what Samantha Lay identifies as a "seaside cycle of films" that has emerged in the 2000s, specifying that "In contemporary social realist film-making the seaside towns of England, long abandoned by the tourists, have become the new symbolic locations of the nation's fragmentation and decay." (Lay 2007)

The cost of caring for asylum seekers fell heavily upon South East seaside resorts. Resentment among local residents in these resorts to the growing immigrant population was evident. By 1998 a local Dover newspaper ran a front page editorial claiming that 'Illegal immigrants, asylum seekers, bootleggers and scum of the earth drug smugglers have targeted our beloved coastline. We are left with the back draft of a nation's human sewage and no cash to wash it down the drain.' *Last Resort* picks up on the effects of the 1999 Immigration and Asylum Act that, apart from introducing a stigmatizing voucher system to replace benefits for asylum seekers, involved an ill-conceived and hurriedly-implemented national dispersal system designed to reduce the concentration of immigrants in the main South East population centres. Tanya's story reflects the ongoing English national examination of identity in a post-imperial age that frequently concentrates on shoring up exaggerated or imagined venerated symbols of municipal pride ('our beloved coastline') and forces that which by its very existence would challenge the orthodoxy to the outer edges of debate (Geddes 2003).

Stonehaven is presented as an unremittingly bleak place; aptly named, it is a barren, grey gulag made carefully reminiscent of what a British audience might imagine Tanya's homeland to be like, although Artiom's description of it as the 'armpit of the Universe' would suggest their new-found home is significantly less appealing than any preconceived post Soviet squalor. There are queues for the one working payphone, a slender lifeline to the outside world, and queues at the fish and chip shop, peddling battered fish with no fish inside the batter. For 'Dreamland' read 'Wasteland'. Stonehaven is a 'designated holding area' characterized by barbed wire fences, ubiquitous surveillance cameras and police canine units patrolling its perimeter. Tanya and Artiom's means of escape is barred, not just by the physical and bureaucratic implements of containment – there are very few vehicles seen in Stonehaven hence their ill-fated attempt to *walk* to London – but also by cultural and linguistic misunderstandings and obstacles.

Pawlikowski's film, not unlike a number of the films discussed in the previous chapter, attempts to find a middle ground between a documentary method with an eye for realist detail and social commentary, and a more dramatic, cinematic approach allowing the viewer to make more humanistic, emotional connections with the story. The result has a more poetic feel than other home-grown social comment tracts that fall back on *cinéma vérité* techniques to drive the authenticity. Amid the constant visual reminders of imprisonment there are interspersed, counterposed shots of huge and beautiful cloudscapes looming over the sea. The alternative view from Tanya and Artiom's flat takes in the curve of the harbour, a lyrical suggestion of beauty and a gateway to escape in opposition to the dilapidated confines of Dreamland. We learn that in Russia Tanya had been a children's book illustrator, and in her boat painting pinned to the wall there is a child-like expression of a longing for salvation and liberty, one that elicits an emotional response from Alfie. It comes as no surprise that a sailing boat features in their eventual escape.

Unlike Tanya, Alfie has seemingly chosen to settle in Stonehaven, as though he has sought and found his own asylum by choice. We learn that he has spent time in prison and there is the suggestion that he had an abusive relationship with his now-deceased father. The backwaters of Stonehaven provide him with a tranquil harbour of sorts, a place where he can put the past behind him and create a new persona, albeit one that initially at least seems to feed upon the sedentary population in much the same way as the town's other exploitative traders. In managing the arcade he is providing the solitary splash of hyperreal colour in the otherwise grey vista, even if in his guise as bingo caller he comes across as the commandant of an over-65s table-top labour camp. But in practically every other respect he is the opposite of Tinker from *The System*; unlike that character Alfie shows little desire to escape Stonehaven, perhaps preferring instead the certainty of its inertia over the uncertainties of the outside world. It is as though the barbed wire is keeping out the forces that might threaten the controllable constancy of his existence. Even though he does not share their desire to leave and initially attempts to convince them to make the best of the bad situation, as he habitually does, Alfie displays a genuine compassion towards Tanya and Artiom's plight. Pawlikowski frequently bathes the character's face in a warm, almost angelic light, suggesting he is a beacon of hope amid the bleakness.

The cyberporn merchant who Tanya turns to in her attempt to raise the money to return to Russia is a prime example of the type of exploitative agency that preys on the vulnerable people drawn to or driven to places like Stonehaven. While it is obviously the case nowadays that the sex and pornography industry has settled into many locales in many different settings, the lure of perceived seaside permissiveness has brought about a distinct exploiter/exploited pattern in the population of a number of prominent resorts, thereby affirming and cementing the seedy reputation of these places.

This is borne out again in two more recent examples that Lay includes with her "seaside cycle": *GYPO* (Jan Dunn 2005) and *Ghosts* (Nick Broomfield 2006). *GYPO* shares much with, indeed owes a debt to, *Last Resort*. It is set amid the desolate off-season gaudiness of Margate, this time not allowed to have its blushes spared courtesy of a rechristening. Dunn employs a documentary visual style, albeit more aligned in tone to the mannered hand-held faux-naturalistic aesthetic of Dogme (in fact this was the first British film to be granted a Dogme95 certificate) than the Loach-esque Brit *Vérité* –meets-skyscape poetry favoured by Pawlikowski, but enlivens the received reality grit with a narrative repeated three times from the perspective of a trio of central characters which serves to emphasize the roots of prejudice and unforeseen compassion. Each of the three 'chapters' is introduced with shots of the characters' names written in pebbles on the beach, a literal and metaphorical spelling out of their predicament, three individuals, the working class couple Helen and Paul stuck in the rut of a loveless marriage and the Czech Romany refugee Tasha on the run along with her mother from a violent husband, all at the mercy of tidal forces, washed up on the shore and marooned, lonely among the many. Which is where *GYPO* differs from *Last Resort*; the three sides of the story are granted equal screen time, and while the apportioning of empathy is not measured out in equal amounts – Paul begins and ends his journey as a dyed-in-the-wool xenophobe - this is a story as much about the residents' response to the presence of refugees in their midst as it is about the refugees themselves. All three are initially stuck in the flypaper of Margate, destined to repeat their day-to-day existence *ad nauseum* in this Groundhog-Day-On-Sea limboland, a point emphasized by the replayed temporal loop of the characters' respective points of view. However all three are granted the liberation that they seek at the denouement; Paul is freed from his fear of change and the sclerosis of the poverty trap that he finds himself in, Helen is unfrozen from the monotony of her life with Paul and allowed to experience a sexual deliverance through her relationship with Tasha, and Tasha herself relinquishes her refugee shackles. In the iconic final shot she literally leaps off the tip of Margate into what we must assume will be a more secure future.

    Broomfield's *Ghosts*, based on the tragic events that led to the deaths of 23 Chinese cockle-pickers in Morecambe Bay in 2004, offers a more stark and bleak depiction of the plight of immigrants eventually mired in the estuarine no man's land, caught between the threats of cultural and tidal eradication. By stepping away from his predominantly documentary back catalogue and into the realm of social realist drama, Broomfield arguably goes further than Pawlikowski in inhabiting his own stylistic middle ground and thereby mirroring the plight of his protagonists' purgatorial state. His *raison d'etre* is also more participative that Pawlikowski's in the sense that *Ghosts* strives further than *Last Resort* to tell not just a sobering political story but to actively change the audience's perception and understanding of the issues involved and encourage them to engage directly with the plight of the protagonists through an appeal on the film's website. *Ghosts* is however more than an exercise in rhetoric, it displays a lyrical storytelling in its construction and an acute sense of symbolism and allusion. Broomfield propels the illegal immigrant characters down the nation's alimentary canal in effect, on a journey through prejudice, exploitation and eventual oblivion in the rising North West tidal waters, consumed, chewed up, spat out. It seems almost inevitable that the Britain that Ai Qin Lin and her compatriots find themselves in will force them through and out of its system like so much effluence onto the hell of Hest Bank.

    Although Morecambe only features briefly at the very beginning, then at length in the final act, it provides Broomfield with the perfect metaphor for his sociopolitical polemic. Not only is it what lies inescapably at the end of his characters' road to perdition, an inevitable terminal netherworld of quicksand and slow death, it also represents the gaudy, unreal promise of wealth and opportunity that brought the migrants to Britain in the first place. Shortly after arrival Ai Qin and her fellow workers spot a welcoming rainbow from the promenade arching over the bay, which they perceive as a sign of hope and a culmination of their shared dream that their hardships will ultimately lead to prosperity and a fruitful return to China. "Home is just on the other side" comments one member of the group, little realizing that it is merely a spectral gateway to their watery grave.

One feature that *Ghosts* shares with *Last Resort* and other texts discussed in this chapter is the presence of sexual exploitation and the so-called 'sex industry' as a quick route out of the central character's predicament. Ai Qin is at one point propositioned by the migrant worker gang leader and has the 'benefits' of working in a massage parlour explained to her as a profitable alternative to the menial farm and factory work she has been shunted into. Unlike Tanya in *Last Resort* Ai Qin refuses to take this path, a decision at least partly influenced by witnessing the indignities tolerated by the gang leader's girlfriend.

This sexual exploitation equation was neatly tapped into in the context of Thatcher's Britain and the politics of sexuality in Phillip Saville's *The Fruit Machine* (1988), yet another seaside-set film that moves between social realism and a form of homespun surrealism, this time in dealing with issues of sexual and racial miscegenation. The central characters Eddie and Michael, two gay Liverpudlian working class teenagers, are compelled to leave their home city, partly because of an abusive family life but largely because as witnesses to a gangland murder they are being pursued. Fate in the form of an invitation from a lecherous aging male opera singer and his vampiric female business associate propel them to Brighton, where Michael is prepared to acquiesce to the sexual advances of *both* of their new 'keepers' in order to protect the more naïve, not yet sexually active Eddie from the same treatment and ensure their cover remains unbroken.

In a sense Eddie and Michael are sexual migrants. Their reasons for leaving Liverpool are underpinned by the potential for sexual and personal self-realization that somewhere like Brighton promises. Julie Burchill's observation of the lure of Brighton sums this up:

> It is a town of runaways, who went as far to the edge of
> England as they could without fleeing into exile, and
> hideaways ... sometimes, in the summer, everyone seems
> young and tall and a brilliant kisser. This is a town where no
> one need go without. (Burchill 2003).

Homelessness statistics for Brighton however do not exactly bear out this promise of successful relocation; a five year study between 1998 and 2002 put the number of rough sleepers in Brighton on a par with, if not greater than, the number recorded in larger, more populous cities like Bristol (Warnes et al 2003).

Other research examining the specific plight of young homeless lesbian, gay and bisexual people suggests that with expanded opportunities for sexual self-expression come increased social risks. While the wider awareness of sexual identity and self-determination became abstractly available to young people since the legal reforms of the 1960s, it did not necessarily lead to a corresponding extension of a social infrastructure to support those left vulnerable by the process of 'coming out', one consequence of which has been a dramatic increase in the number of homeless gay people nationally (Dunne et al 2002). The year of *The Fruit Machine*'s release saw the enactment of the controversial Section 28 amendment to the Local Government Act, which sought to contain the promotion of homosexuality through publishing and teaching. In this climate it is possible to read into the film a sense that its protagonists are being hounded to the outer edges and thenceforth exploited not simply by the gangland assassin on their tail but also by the opinions prevalent in government and wider society.

The Fruit Machine is primarily Eddie's odyssey and one that is suffused with surrealism; his memories of an earlier family holiday in Brighton, in particular surrounding the dolphins at the Wonderland aquarium, shape his ambitions. Being gay and of mixed race he sees in the dolphins an expression of desirable otherness, sentient creatures capable of bonding with humans and offering seemingly unconditional love. He even fantasizes that his 'ideal man' can sometimes take the form of a dolphin. To Eddie they embody uncorrupted perfection and are a projection of free will beyond prejudice. Ben Gove notes how Eddie 'feels an increasing connection between his own marginalized cultural position and that of the captive dolphins' (Gove 1996: 186). When he revisits the aquarium he is upset to witness their performance which is seemingly designed to titillate the audience. One of the dolphins has been trained to remove its female trainer's top to reveal her breasts, a sight that fuels Eddie's anger that his object of unconstrained hope has been forced into an overtly heterosexualised role. Later in the film Eddie returns to the aquarium at night and swims with the dolphins. This is a climactic, sexual baptism; when Eddie breaks the skin of the water in the pool he symbolically passes through the skin that separates the worlds of innocent naturalness and adolescent desire. Although probably coincidental, there is also a brief scene in *Last Resort* of Artiom watching a wildlife television documentary featuring dolphins. Here too the dolphins, shown mating, offer the young but developing boy a glimpse of the world of adult desires, with only the thickness of the television screen separating him from it.

Brighton's association with criminality and exploitation was in part reinforced by Graham Greene's 1938 novel *Brighton Rock*, filmed nine years later by John Boulting. *Brighton Rock* is essentially an observation of the amorality and exploitative tendencies of a disaffected, pessimistic, manipulative teenage racketeer defending his territory at a seaside resort, a character description superficially similar to that of *The System*'s Tinker. However, Pinkie Brown is a significantly more sadistic, violent and nihilistic protagonist. Greene described as a 'fallen angel', one who believes himself already damned; 'Of course there's a Hell…flames, damnations, torments' he tells the young apparatchik Rose, as he unconsciously wraps her rosary around his fingers in the manner of a garrotte. In this sense Brighton doubles as the brink of a Hadean abyss (Pinkie's telephone number being "*three sixes* and a five"), a meaning reinforced in the film by the number of violent deaths involving individuals falling from a height.

Again unlike *The System*'s Tinker, Pinkie is a native of the town, as it would seem are all the main players except his main gangland rival Colleoni. Pinkie's otherness comes from his Catholicism, placing him *in* the world of Brighton but not *of* it. Pinkie is set apart from the seediness of Brighton; as Jake Arnott observed 'Evil he may be, but pure of mundane pleasures and cheap thrills' (Arnott 2002). However there is no sense that Pinkie aspires to escape Brighton's confines, indeed Brighton is the extent of the seventeen-year-old Pinkie's world, one that he seeks only to control and command. The cold-hearted cruelty that he employs in dealing with those who would cross him is not simply a product of his desire to rule at all costs. The jealousy and paranoia that define his character belie a sexual inadequacy and anxiety, despite his awareness that a professed sexual potency is a necessary part of maintaining his position as gang leader and local kingpin aspirant. The other members of his gang are all rendered physically or psychologically weak, or wear staid suits compared to his sharp attire, allowing the baby-faced Pinkie to hold the upper hand among them. From this artificial position of strength Pinkie not only spreads fear but also experiences fear himself. This is partly an Oedipal fear of castration embodied by his opponent Colleoni and his razor gang. The main danger to Pinkie is however not so much the castrating father figure as the devouring mother. The females who might inform on or uncover him pose a greater threat. Ida Arnold the brassy, middle-aged entertainer primarily possesses a blousy, maternal conviviality and her evident belief in life as a process of enjoying every sensual pleasure is not simply the opposite of Pinkie's mean-spirited world view, it represents the subversive threat to every system or notion of masculine identity and order that he cleaves to. Ida rapidly becomes the prevailing force that threatens to disclose Pinkie's intentions, initially through her rudimentary bar-room divination – a route for mere mortals to contact the Underworld perhaps – and later in her role as amateur sleuth and avenging angel.

There are many metaphysical meditations upon the symbioses between land/sea, man/woman and heaven/hell running throughout *Brighton Rock*. Pinkie's fear of being consumed by the result of what springs from the mouths of female informants is reminiscent of the encroachment by the female tide upon the male shore. Indeed this notion of being 'swallowed up' presents the greater threat of emasculation. An early scene shows Pinkie leaning over the balustrade of the Palace Pier studying the action of the tide upon the pier's legs, suggesting the threat of consumption or erosion of the masculine land by the feminine sea, reflecting Pinkie's fear of drowning as highlighted in the novel and foreshadowing his eventual fate.

The pier is emblematic of phallic conceit, an audacious 'man-made' promontory extending out into the lapping waters, it is the platform on which Pinkie in his circumstance of otherness is deposited, develops and dies; we learn in the novel that he was first found 'coughing on the Palace Pier in the bitter cold' by the veteran gangster Kite whom he would succeed, as though Pinkie 'the Other' was born of this place, neither of the mainland nor the deep. He metes out his own justice upon Hale, the man Pinkie's gang regard as responsible for Kite's death, whom he throws from a car on the pier's ghost train ride into the tide below. His relationship with Rose develops during numerous meetings on the pier, notably when she coaxes him into making a recording of his voice for posterity as a wedding present using a recording booth situated in the pier's amusement arcade.

The windows of the booth are one of a number of significantly non-permeable glass or reflective surfaces in both the novel and the film. These are in part symbolic of the separating and isolating surface between the aforementioned land/sea dualities, a meniscus through which possibly only Pinkie can see and consequently a threshold which he fears to cross. His ability to see through and beyond the skin of Brighton further separates Pinkie from the mere mortals he walks among. There are several references to the partial or total blindness of other characters, sometimes manifesting as a metaphorical blindness as in Ida's inability to see beyond the façade of Brighton's material pleasures compared to Pinkie's knowledge of the ugly 'real' Brighton. Rose is certainly blind to Pinkie's characters traits and intentions. She looks on lovingly and obliviously as he records his message of hate within the glazed protection of the pier's recording booth. Furthermore it is tempting to interpolate, when we are shown his vantage point in Snow's seafront café where he first meets Rose and observes the ambulance removing the murdered Hale, whether only Pinkie can see the word 'Sodas' written on the outside of the café window and read meaning into its reversed form 'sados'.

This notion of the seaside setting as a thin film separating two states of being is explored further in Michael Winterbottom's *I Want You* (1998). Although it is a comparatively simplistic text and one that arguably fails to fully realize its themes, *I Want You* starkly places its action directly in this diaphanous realm between solid and liquid elements. Daytime exterior shots of the beach and promenade at the fictional Farhaven (the film was shot in Hastings) are bathed in an unnatural sulfurous yellow light, giving the locale a purgatorial complexion, one reminiscent of aspic or amber in which the characters are trapped. An early parallel between fossils hewn from the local rocks and the predicament of Farhaven's inhabitants encased in its resinous margin emphasizes this.

There are numerous analogies of otherness and separation to be found; characters possess a broad mix of accents, including Irish and Scottish, suggesting much regional and national displacement to Farhaven. Honda, a young Eastern European immigrant, and his older sister Smokey inhabit a dilapidated beach house set apart from the town. Smokey exercises her Catholicism and her sexual appetite with equal fervour, forging her energies as a nightclub singer on the isolation of the stage, enveloped in an otherworldly, blue aquatic light. Honda has been rendered mute by the death of his parents and attempts to make contact with the world with an array of listening devices and recording equipment. It is as though he is holding an ear up to the thin barrier that separates him from the world; at one point he uses an electronic ear to penetrate the fly-specked windscreen of a car and hear its occupants, at another he is pressed against the thick glass in an aquarium attempting to detect the sounds of the creatures on the other side of the thickened glass. He even sticks microphones to a beachfront apartment window in order to listen to the conversation within, a metaphorical identification, acknowledgement and attempted penetration of the dividing 'skin'. Several brief distorted replays of earlier scenes seen from the point of view of Honda's mind's eye punctuate the film, seemingly shot through a thickened, gelated lens to further emphasize the clotted, hermetic nature of Farhaven.

Honda forms a platonic relationship with Helen, a more mature local hairdresser and central player in the film's concurrent plot thread. Beyond his initial innocent infatuation with her, Honda's bond of fellowship with Helen is founded around their shared otherness as orphans. Helen herself exists on the fringes of Farhaven, stigmatized by her involvement in the murder of her father. Martin, being the man convicted of the murder, is also regarded as Other. He reenters the cataract of Farhaven at the film's outset and proceeds to obsessively stalk Helen, his former lover. He is psychologically damaged by his term of imprisonment and returns seeking a tangled combination of revenge and redemption from Helen for taking the blame and serving time for the murder that she in fact committed. Their first onscreen encounter upon his return sees Martin save Helen from an attempted rape outside the nightclub on Farhaven's pier, a moment that graphically revisits some of the themes associated with the pier in *Brighton Rock*. At night the pier becomes the penetrative causeway audaciously conjoining solid with liquid and is territorialized by predatory sexual forces afforded a right to roam by its permissive, transitional corridor.

The climactic scenes of Neil Jordan's *Mona Lisa* (1986) offer a further illustration of the drama of otherness played out through transgressions of the elemental crossing point provided by a coastal resort. Even before the Brighton-set final act the film shares much with the texts already discussed; through the character of Simone the mixed race, sexually ambiguous call-girl there are considerations of racial, sexual and class-related passage and the divide between states that she inhabits. *Mona Lisa* is a film defined by the maintenance and eventual collapse of surfaces, masks and artifice. George, a small time criminal recently released from jail, becomes fascinated by and attempts to penetrate Simone's Mona Lisa-esque 'veneer'. Furthermore the illusory pretense of Brighton is foreshadowed by the comfort that George derives from the clichés of storytelling that the banter with his friend Thomas provides. Thomas deals in suitably tacky simulacra – kitsch Virgin Mary lamps and plastic sculptures of plates of realistic but inedible spaghetti – and the two converse in terms of fantastical pulp crime fiction logic. George carries this into his hopes of forging a relationship with Simone, even asking at one point if she is familiar with the fairy tale of the frog prince.

George and Simone's journey culminates at Brighton, specifically in a scene that takes place on the Palace Pier during which George's illusions are shattered when Simone admits to her lesbianism. The pier environment facilitates the revelation; it is as though this headland construct stretching out beyond the protective veneer of the resort allows matters to literally come to a head. In the panic of the threat that this realization poses to the façade that he has constructed, George resorts to disguising himself and Simone with pairs of cheap, novelty sunglasses in order to desperately maintain the masque he wishes to perform. He proceeds to play out a crude, brutish pantomime of what he perceives as 'normal' behaviour for a couple strolling along the pier, as he attempts to explain:

> …we're on holiday ain't we…We're meant to have fun, like men and women do…They have fun, they walk arm in arm you know…Cos they love each other and they get married so they can love each other more and have a little baby,

only a little one…And have fights with the fucking mother-in-law…You know the way it is, between men and fucking women…

The walk on the pier provided the catalyst to the collapse of George's world and it is in this vulnerable state that he reverts to short bursts of violence in disposing of the gang of thugs sent by Simone's former pimp to track the pair down. The events on the pier bring him uncomfortably close to the surface that separates his fantasy from reality, the horizon that divides his feelings for Simone from her unattainability, and the violence is his attempt to punch through that surface. Amid the fracas Jordan inserts a shot of a troupe of dwarf entertainers comically reenacting the kicks, punches and head butts that George administers to his assailants, as though the inhabitants of the surface that he is now so close to mock George with a funhouse mirror reflection of his actions.

As with Alfie's attack on the seafront cyberporn premises in *Last Resort* and Martin's beating of Helen's attacker on the pier in *I Want You*, George's actions are defensive but born of a release of almost primeval emotional pressure and frustration made possible by his temporary suspension from terra firma when on the pier. It is perhaps an example of what Urbain describes as the 'reprimitivization' of the seaside, the process linked to the relaxing of behavioural permissions in the Twentieth Century discussed in chapter one, that appropriates what he regards as a 'restoration of wildness to the shore' (Urbain 2003: 113). The violence is perhaps part of the same stripping back of the complexities of urban life that has resulted in the widespread consumption of food with the hands in public, the abandonment of everyday clothing or even nudity and the alcohol-fuelled debauchery now seemingly integral to the British seaside experience. Linked to this primal elemental aesthetic George experiences a form of death (submersion) and revival (re-emergence) when passing through the experiential threshold represented by the events on the pier.

Paul Andrew Williams' *London To Brighton* (2006), another of Lay's 'seaside cycle' of films, follows both geographically and spiritually in the footsteps of *Mona Lisa*. Both thrillers concern a prostitute and her young ward who flee to the coast, only to find that it's not so nice to be beside the seaside. From the outset runaway Joanne is deposited in a series of havens of filth, from the opening scene in a toilet cubicle to the grubby train carriage out of

London and eventually the environs of Brighton itself. This is again a Hadean Brighton of lost souls; the not-so-safe house that Kelly the prostitute takes Joanne to is populated exclusively by recumbent dopeheads suspended in their anaesthetizing fug. The two fleeing females and more particularly the pimp and his associate who pursue them puncture this narcosis with their urgency and violence. Lay picks up on the explosive contrast and incisive effect that travelers from the capital can have on the seaside town:

> Its London-by-the-sea reputation and the criminal inferences this brings, means that films set in Brighton often incorporate themes and issues that revolve around criminality and the pernicious effects of Londoners and London life...The London connection adds a cosmopolitan frisson which contrasts with the melancholic, reflective overtones of the British seascape. (ibid)

The sense that this is as far as Kelly and Joanne can go in escaping their pursuers, emphasized by shots of the two females staring at the finality of the sea, heightens the palpable dread, but this is more than a dead end. Brighton is young runaway Joanne's *mandorla*, the liminal overlap of adolescence between the heaven/hell worlds of childhood and adulthood that she is violently ushered into. Amid its out-of-season desolation pinpricks of pure light and colour illuminate her passage between the two states. The brightly lit Palace Pier amusement arcade offers a brief respite from the gloom, a cuddly-toy-grabbing crane depositing a last reminder of Joanne's childish playfulness (ironically in this social realist film Joanne's success in actually managing to grab a cuddly toy with this machine provides the least believably realistic moment!) before she is propelled further into the violent grown-up world. A brief montage showing the pimp cradling a fearsome firearm echoed in the next moment by a shot of Joanne holding and swinging on a coin-operated telescope on the sea front perhaps foreshadows the twelve-year-old's violent shift from simple juvenile pleasures to terrifying adult decisions – she will be forced to weald the same firearm in the film's denouement. Upon arriving at the sea front Joanne cannot resist taking a dip into the icy tide. This not only symbolizes her attempt to wash away the filth and the memory of the sex act and murder we come to learn she was forced into before fleeing the capital, but also signifies the short, sharp and shocking baptismal events to come.

The theme of adolescent rebirth or revivification is brought to the fore in Mark Herman's *Little Voice* (1998). The character of LV undergoes perhaps the purest and most manifestly wrought expression of incarceration and liberation of any character so far discussed. Herman's relocation of Jim Cartwright's 1992 play *The Rise and Fall of Little Voice* from an unspecified Northern industrial town to an out-of-season Scarborough may have been expediently intended to avoid comparisons with *The Full Monty* (Peter Cattaneo 1997) and Herman's previous film *Brassed Off* (1996), but the emergence of the reticent, reclusive, almost speechless LV through the obstructive gauze of vulgarity represented by her foul-mouthed, hard-drinking and loveless mother into the temporary spotlight of fame is well suited to this seaside resort. Its air of gloom and faded glamour lends itself to the main character's glitzy emergence from the everyday. As the director indicated in interview:

> …we chose this place called Scarborough, which is a seaside holiday resort in the north of England. And it adds another character to the film…I was brought up in a little town which is just south of where we shot. I used to love the off season, when all the holiday makers go home and you've just got a dead town. (Rabinowitz 1998)

Beneath the obvious social separation, LV experiences a cultural otherness in Scarborough, her singing talent marking her out as clearly different from the people around her. The town grips its inhabitants in a stereotypically 'grim up North' stranglehold, enveloping and weighing down on them like a sea-spray dampened overcoat, keeping them parochial, embittered and belligerent. LV has retreated to her spartan bedroom eyrie and seeks solace through the playing of her deceased father's record collection, upstairs and away from the town's almost preternaturally drab back streets as much as from her mother's crass, degenerate downstairs spaces.

Scarborough also provides the kitsch seafront nightclub where LV temporarily transcends her corporeal restraints and through her stage performance, mimicking Garland, Monroe, Bassey and others, manages to break open the doors of her cage and push through the barriers that have contained her.

LV's age is not specified but her isolation holds her in a spell of suspended pre-adolescence. When the spell is broken and she finds her own true voice she rapidly passes through into a more natural adolescence, but in her isolation LV has come to obsessively idolize her father. There is a feeling that their relationship may have verged on incestuous, although given the pantheon of torch singers that make up her father's taste in music one could just as easily surmise that this is the spirit of gay man living on through his daughter, initially closeted, eventually fabulous. LV remains connected to him through the playing of his record collection and regurgitating the songs – including 'My Heart Belongs To Daddy' - is her way of communicating with him and maintaining the link. His shrine-like photograph on the wall of her room and his ghostly appearances at important moments in the story, notably as a face in the audience on her first night, give LV hope that there is a world beyond her confines, as the lyrics of Garland's 'Get Happy' suggest:

> We're headin' 'cross the river
>
> Wash your sins away in the tide
>
> It's oh, so peaceful
>
> On the other side

The relationship between the seaside and the world of entertainment is revisited in the next chapter, in its reflection of post-imperial decline.

Chapter three: End of the pier show?

> Of all Blackpool's performers, the one I like best is the poor old rector of Stiffkey…he had himself roasted in a glass oven while a mechanical demon prodded him with a pitchfork. These days, by way of torture, Blackpool contents itself with Jim Davidson, Little and Large, Keith Harris and Orville and Bernard Manning. How much would you pay to see any one of them roasted in an oven?
>
> Charles Jennings: *Up North: travels beyond the Watford Gap.*
> London : Little, Brown, 1995

This chapter will concentrate on a number of seaside-set films made in the post war years that in part reflect the nation's post-imperial decline during this period. Some of the texts discussed share a depiction of the seaside resort as an anachronistic, faded relic of a former time, either to hark back nostalgically to some imagined pre war golden age or to illustrate the sense of decay, loss and social disenfranchisement particularly prevalent in the 1960s.

The more recently made films to feature in the chapter pick up on and mirror the partial revival of fortunes of resorts as sites of quintessentially eccentric national character. Seaside resorts since the 1950s have been all too easily categorized by social commentators as worn out and anachronistic, as this example demonstrates:

> … decaying confections of fantastical architecture, rotting art deco, the dance hall glitterball and the ornamental balustrade… faded grandeur abutting sea-front dereliction… affordable, exotic, alternately camp and luxuriously sad - a kind of gilded social realism…English seaside towns have developed an allegorical identity - a mood of acute romanticism in which they recollect their past within their present. (Bracewell 2004)

But this tone fails to acknowledge that there is succor to be derived from the capacity for reinvention and the ability to synthesize a cultural past and present that many resorts possess.

Lindsey Anderson's *O Dreamland* made in 1953, although a small and highly personal work, is historiographically pertinent to the discussion and can now be regarded as culturally emblematic of the post war demise of a national identity founded on notions of Empire. Its representation of the dilapidation of Margate's seafront practically illustrated a fraying at the edges of the old Home Front, as though the geographical delineation that both bound the people of the island together and repelled external forces had developed an irreversible porousness. Anderson and the other protagonists of the Free Cinema movement would go on to make major contributions to the new wave of social Realist Cinema in the late 1950s and early 1960s with its emphasis on post-imperial decline, and it is in this climate that the majority of the films discussed in this chapter were made.

In the immediate post war period and prior to the making of *O Dreamland* the consensual camaraderie captured by the bulk of Ealing Studios' output continued to draw upon the notions of social cohesion born of a shared austerity and nostalgia for the pre war and wartime years, whilst shunning external elements of change. Films like *Passport to Pimlico* (Henry Cornelius 1949) and *The Titfield Thunderbolt* (Charles Crichton 1952) reiterated gentler patrician values in the face of growing corporatisation and 'Americanisation'. Charles Frend's *Barnacle Bill* (1957) runs the gamut of Ealing's multitude of thematic and stylistic motifs. Therefore it comes as no surprise that, after previous comedies based around such typically eccentric yesteryear icons as a steam train in *The Titfield Thunderbolt*, a vintage car in the Rank-produced Ealing-esque *Genevieve* (Henry Cornelius 1953) and a coal powered boat in *The Maggie* (Alexander Mackendrick 1954), the studio should eventually set a story on a crumbling 1000 foot long Victorian pier, in this case at the prim, fictional Sandcastle-On-Sea (the pier at Hunstanton was used for the location work). In the case of the pier in *Barnacle Bill* the nostalgic transport thread is maintained by having its owner, William Horatio Ambrose played by Alec Guinness, register it as a 'ship' and conduct 'cruises' by way of upholding his family maritime heritage and navigating around his own seasickness. Ambrose's last stand against the local authorities, who want to seize and condemn the decrepit building, is also in line with the typical Ealing scenario of the little man taking on the starchy bureaucrats, as in *Passport to Pimlico* and others.

But this is a benign, comfortable subversiveness from a world view that Jeffrey Richards described as 'essentially quaint, cosy, whimsical and backward-looking' (Richards 1999: 151). A distinction here is that what passed for pluck and stoicism in *Passport To Pimlico* seems more like blinkered insularity in *Barnacle Bill*. Whereas the Burgundian secession in *Passport To Pimlico* is born out of the same Atlee era positive ethos of social unity as *Holiday Camp*, by 1957 the same message in *Barnacle Bill* feels out of touch with the social changes of the period. Ambrose repels the land as much as the sea by declaring the pier a sea-going vessel, effectively creating his own private island of Middle English small insular values reacting to change going on around it, happier being cut off. Regarded as the last of the Ealing comedies, it is literally straying from the centre of Michael Balcon's post war Ealing criteria of 'building up of a native [film industry] with its roots firmly planted in the soil of this country' (Balcon 1969: 48). The film perhaps inadvertently presents such values as metaphorically cut adrift and certainly translates as anachronistic at its time of release.

Barnacle Bill's superannuated principles become particularly apparent when contrasted with John Osborne's play *The Entertainer*, written and first performed in 1957 and later filmed by Tony Richardson in 1960. *The Entertainer* uses the metaphor of the dying music hall tradition to comment on Britain's general post war decline, its loss of its Empire, its power, and its cultural confidence and identity, something flagrantly revealed during the Suez Crisis of November 1956 which elliptically forms the backdrop to the play.

If anything, by the time of the film's release the impression of the seaside resort and the traditional English seaside holiday as the epitome of all things jaded and unfashionable was even more pronounced. The Morecambe of the filmed version of *The Entertainer* is one based upon director Richardson's own memories of childhood holidays spent there, a place that he described as 'a failed popular resort with decaying piers and crumbling theatres, the second-class sister to the livelier, more raucous, still-popular Blackpool' where he passed the time 'hating the concrete pavements, the mean boarding houses, the vulgarity of the restaurants and shows' (Richardson 1993: 138). The resort once again represents Purgatory, this time one that mimics the national sclerosis and lack of direction.

The Entertainer is a bitter reflection of the angry, cynical sentiments that defined post war Britain and a repudiation of earlier films that portrayed entertainers and their industry as one long parade of sunshine and good will. Instead of a parade, *The Entertainer* is a funeral, and inherent in the film's depiction of dwindling glory is an indictment of Britain's dying prestige. The film also marked a turning point for Laurence Olivier, whose performance as the washed up Song and Dance Man Archie Rice was a departure from his earlier roles. The casting of Olivier in both the original theatrical run and the film is highly significant. When Olivier played Henry V at the time of national wartime unity, Charles Laughton remarked: 'Do you know why you're so good in this part? Because you *are* England, that's all.' (quoted in Holden 1988: 172), a sentiment that illustrates how Olivier could so readily embody England's post-imperial shame. Rice's hollow self-delusion, hypocrisy, misanthropy, his fiscal and moral bankruptcy and clear lack of talent mirrors the arrogance and misplaced confidence of society at that time.

The traditional Victorian Punch and Judy show, so much an ingredient of the collectively perceived idea of the seaside holiday, became particularly and somewhat unfairly synonymous with bygone times in the second half of the twentieth century, especially when seen to be competing with the emerging visual lure of television in the 1950s and 1960s. Having already admitted that his form of beach entertainment is being killed off by television, Wally Pinner the despairing puppeteer in *The Punch and Judy Man* (Jeremy Summers 1963) wryly passes judgment upon the opposition midway through a show during one of Mr. Punch's typically murderous parenting episodes. When asked if he watches much television he replies 'Nah, too much violence. Bad for the kids.' The world is changing while Pinner crouches in his beach tent, and while not oblivious to this change he receives it largely with a morbid resignation.

Pinner's dwindling puppet show audiences represent the draining away of emphasis on the was of the past and by extension the dominion once enjoyed by the imperial value system that such entertainments sprang from and came to embody. For Pinner and his ilk the show is almost over and they face a future of redundancy, both actual and spiritual. In discussing *The Punch and Judy Man* its star Tony Hancock, who was raised in Bournemouth, reflected on the motive behind the setting of the film and the character of the children's entertainer:

> Being brought up in a seaside town, you find these poor, underground entertainers who are absolutely honest. You may say they're finished…Every time I go to a seaside town I find these underground people, maybe a Punch and Judy man, a dedicated man to his own trade, for what else can he do? (Films and Filming 1962: 11)

As a rearguard action Pinner rails against the snobbery and petty bureaucracy of the resort's councillors who appear driven by avarice and self-aggrandizement to apply a superficial modern gloss to the town and remove old-fashioned elements such as Pinner and his beach entertainer cronies. Shot at Bognor Regis, the film is set in the fictional Piltdown Bay, a place name that unsubtly comments on the fallaciousness of its civic leaders and social climbers with its obvious parallel to the artifice of the Piltdown Man hoax that was uncovered in the early 1950s.

The tone of Pinner's conflict with modernity in *The Punch and Judy Man* is pessimistic and downbeat, which contrasts with Ambrose's whimsical head-in-the-sand detachment in *Barnacle Bill*. In doing battle with the forces of change there is an underlying sense that the likes of Pinner are a dying breed who will ultimately lose the argument and have to either shut up or ship out. Pinner is left to score cheap points against the agents of change, employing small time anarchy and cocking a snook in the manner of Mr. Punch himself. Despite his best efforts there is no real suggestion that the stand he takes against the status seekers in his midst will be successful. Indeed the sense of an unstoppable process of erosion, at personal, socio-cultural and national levels, is palpable. It is reflected in the worn-out confines of the end-of-season Piltdown and also finds an expression in Pinner's stagnating marriage. This is a childless couple trapped in a decaying relationship and kept together purely by force of habit – for what else can they do? – whose domestic fragmentation is pointedly played out over an early scene of petty matrimonial annoyances at the breakfast table. Pinner is reduced to sublimating his marital and professional frustrations through the brutality of the Punch play and his skirmishes with the local legislature, a neurosis that distracts him from the gradual disappearance of his marriage, livelihood and surroundings.

The erosion of Pinner's and Piltdown's *raison d'être*, particularly in the face of competition from the emerging continental holiday market with its promise of unlimited sun and uninhibited fun, is illustrated by a passage set during a torrential rainstorm that leaves the promenade practically depopulated save for one small boy, Pinner's lone fan, who he treats to a knickerbocker glory in a seafront ice cream parlour. By ingratiating the boy Pinner is clinging despairingly to the slender reed of hope that he represents now that the holiday crowds have been washed away. The next scene, featuring Pinner's equally desperate compatriots left to play on the pinball machines and other arcade amusements in the total absence of holidaymakers, emphasizes the feeling that the carnival is over.

In his 1969 film version of Joan Littlewood's 1963 satirical stage musical *Oh! What a Lovely War*, Richard Attenborough shifted the focal point of the drama from the Big Top circus tent of the play to Brighton's West Pier. The pier afforded a more cinematic encapsulation of the nation at the time of World War One, complete with the appropriate illuminated sign above its entrance, and was if anything an even more effective manifestation of the absurd, obstinate conceit of the campaign's military leaders and the futility of their 'game of war' and War in general. The combination of the soldiers' haunting marching songs and the scenes of British subjects entering through the pier's turnstiles with Field Marshal Haig as the ticket master tartly illustrate the cynical herding of popular opinion, the tragic, orchestrated lemming-like parade off the metaphorical gangplank of the pier into oblivion and the subsequent collapse of national optimism as the war years progress.

Even compared to the films already discussed in this chapter, *Oh! What a Lovely War* is inextricably a product of its time. Although a period piece it is firmly rooted in the politics of the 1960s and sparked an examination of the motives of combat and maintenance of the Stiff Upper Lip, as Dan Todman describes:

> In the aftermath of the Second World War, and under the shadow of the atomic bomb and the arms race, a generation had grown up whose attitudes were uniquely anti-authority and anti-war. It did not matter what they were shown or

told; their reaction to the idea of war was that it was horrific and futile. (Todman 2002: 30)

Littlewood's 1963 stage version reflected and tapped into the tumultuous social changes and growing anti-war movement of the time. By 1969 the immediate lineage and political resonance of Attenborough's film was unambiguous; in terms of British film Joseph Losey's *King & Country* (1964), being based on a stage play about trench desertion that comments on class injustices and the insanity of war, is a direct although markedly more intimate antecedent. The anti-war sentiment told through black comedy had also been present in Richard Lester's *How I Won The War* (1967) and to a large extent in the same director's post-nuclear *The Bed-Sitting Room* (1969). *Oh! What a Lovely War* plays very much as a reaction to the ongoing Vietnam War, but by portraying the Home Front amid Brighton's naturally characteristic mixture of surreal fantasy-meets-reality and faded grandeur Attenborough was able to communicate a broad allegory to all wars, their attendant crumbling regimes and the sharp experiential contrast between the domestic reception of war and combat itself. A shot that typifies this features the fantastical transposition of a character dressed in civilian clothes from one of the pier's shooting galleries to the trenches where he is now in uniform. Alan Burton describes how the shot focuses on the gun during the interchange enacting 'a shift in perspective from carefree amusement to deadly earnest combat' (Burton 2002: 38-39)

Based on the decay and collapse of pre war values reflected in the depictions of resorts and their characters in the texts discussed in this chapter one might expect to be able to chart an inexorable decline in the perceived national identity through similar projects up to present day. However this would be to deny the point that John Walton makes in discussing the capacity for reinvention that many resorts possess, a reinvention and indomitability that has found an expression through a number of films in recent years. Walton argues that the British seaside has displayed resilience in the face of external competition and economic downturn:

> …it has maintained its power as a cultural referent, and is beginning to market itself in post-modern ironic ways, inviting visitors to share the jokes about seaside kitsch and enjoy a distinctive experience…There is still plenty of life in

the enduring and reinvented traditions and the continuing openness to innovation... (Walton 2000: 198)

One text that successfully reflected this opinion whilst also retaining and celebrating the traditional comprehension of resort life and accentuating the eccentricity of seaside inhabitants was Peter Chelsom's Blackpool-set *Funny Bones* (1995). Chelsom draws a parallel between the resort and Las Vegas in the film's plot about Tommy Fawkes, an up-and-coming comedian who bombs spectacularly on the Vegas stage and flees to Blackpool to seek out the source of his father's comic success. While Blackpool's peculiarly tatty Englishness is not shied away from, its comparative warmth emerges. Andy Medhurst regards Blackpool as 'a funny-bones resort, belching excess from every pore' and describes Chelsom's film as 'a love letter to Blackpool's unrepentant seaside culture' (Medhurst 1995: 9).

This love and warmth is in evidence in its depiction of some of the resident entertainers who emerge when word gets around that an American entrepreneur is in town. The audition sequence that follows features a Fellini-esque parade of real eccentrics, from a unicyclist in drag to a singing dog to a musical saw act, what Medhurst refers to as a 'Rabelasian *Opportunity Knocks*' (ibid: 7). The acts are more than simply representative of the local community, they have absorbed the surreal spirit of the place.

Fawkes' personal journey is one of a rediscovery of meaning. It is also defined by the disassembling of cynicism that Blackpool provokes, allowing him to embrace truths about himself. We learn that he has happy childhood memories of Blackpool, and by returning there he undergoes a transformation. He returns home and is reborn, having realised that humour is not a marketable commodity, and this transformative process is made possible largely by those unquantifiable cultural elements of the Blackpool experience that Nicola Kirkham picks up on in her analysis of *Funny Bones*:

> The town of Blackpool is not a scientific object, that is, its meaning cannot be located purely within either its physical or cultural materialisations, such as its population surveys or maps, but only from within the context of culturally, historically and spatially specific information. (Kirkham 2003: 72)

The journey taken by Andrew Kötting in the making of his patchwork travelogue *Gallivant* (1998) was equally transformative and celebratory. Beginning and ending at Bexhill-on-Sea, Kötting, his grandmother Gladys and his daughter Eden travel together around the entire 6000 mile coastline of mainland Britain. Throughout their journey they meet a host of likeable, genial and frequently eccentric inhabitants on the fringes of the land, and in the process get to know each other. The need for this belated acquaintance is heightened by the knowledge that both Gladys and Eden have limited life expectancy. Gladys is drawing to the end of her days and Eden has the neurological condition Joubert Syndrome. In filming his family members undertaking this journey Kötting managed to capture an unsentimentalised yet affirming and personal pilgrimage shot through with touching intimacy. *Gallivant*'s language is the family seaside holiday home movie made manifest; its visual aesthetic is all Super 8 sans synch speech, primary colour picture postcard cut-ups interspersed with black and white jump cuts, flits between video and film, tripod and hand-held, in what Ian Sinclair described as an 'idiot cubism' (Sinclair 1998: 20).

As with *Funny Bones* it is the succession of idiosyncratic local people that Kötting encounters in the coastal towns and wilds that gives the film its warmth and democracy. Gareth Evans' opinion of *Gallivant* in his profile of the director bears this out:

> It has a wide ear and eye, both for folk, their ways and for signage, for the scale sweep and the sweet stall. It makes the personal a generous filter into the social. It understands the switchback exchange between the two. Deeply, it belongs. (Evans 2005)

Amid the flickbook of found moments Kötting pauses to persuade some of the locals variously to remember the words to the song 'John Peel', display their bunions, show off their best gurning face, and in the case of one John Conolly, this writer's brother, roll up his trouser legs, strap on his accordion and deliver a whiskery sea shanty while slowly sinking into the sand at Cleethorpes.

Kötting deals in what Evans calls 'the littoral truths of this island' (ibid); rather than use cosy, familiar icons of Nation-On-Sea as his currency of communication (save for occasional shots such as the beach huts at Bexhill that recall John Betjeman) he chooses to look the Land in the face and speak as he finds. It would not be unreasonable to wonder why Kötting could not have simply opted for a more straightforward, logistical A to B journey. But this is an odyssey of understanding, a circuit of enlightenment. Only by completing his circumnavigation, by probing the nooks and crannies of the country's beached margin, can Kötting capture the essence of his homeland and come to know his family and himself.

Conclusion: "Somewhere spoilt"

> Trudging slowly over wet sand
> Back to the bench where your clothes were stolen
> This is the coastal town
> That they forgot to close down
> Armageddon - come armageddon!
> Come, armageddon! come!
>
> Stephen Morrissey: Lyrics: *Every day is like Sunday*. Viva Hate
> HMV (UK), 1988

The trajectory of this book has taken in many aspects of the British seaside resort experience as reflected on film. The hope is that these and the numerous other seaside-set films not featured can be viewed as a distinct grouping that have the capacity to carry clearly wrought socio-cultural commentary and allegory as well as capturing the metaphorical significance of resort spaces.

In concluding it is important to draw attention to and account for aspects that have been omitted from the preceding chapters. Television productions based around seaside themes, primarily from the 1970s and 1980s, have not featured, largely for reasons of brevity but essentially because the differences in cultural reception of television programmes would have led to a discontinuous stylistic narrative. These programmes would potentially form the basis for a companion piece of research, but there is value in providing a brief overview here to account for the historical gap.

The decline in interest in British seaside resorts as holiday destinations during 1970s and 1980s, due largely to the growth of continental package holidays, was mirrored by a sharp lack of seaside based British feature films over the same period, not necessarily directly related as overall British film output at this time was in decline, but noteworthy nonetheless. In these intervening years television would begin to equate the seaside holiday with nostalgia, particularly for the old-fashioned bawdiness of the postcards of Donald McGill and his ilk – see such productions as the Two Ronnies' *By The Sea* (BBC, 1982) and innumerable seaside-based sketches on *The Benny Hill Show* (ITV, 1969-1989) – and also for the happy (or otherwise) memories of post-war leisure embodied by holiday camps, represented almost exclusively by Jimmy Perry and David Croft's *Hi-De-Hi* (BBC, 1980-1988). The spectre of Torquay's *Fawlty Towers* (BBC, 1975-1979) also naturally looms large over any discussion of television and the depiction of social class during this period.

In addition two single television dramas from this period stand out as worthy of further attention because of their relation to many of the themes raised in discussion of the other film texts in this dissertation. *All Day On The Sands* (BBC, 1979) written by Alan Bennett and *East Of Ipswich* (BBC, 1987) written initially as a play by Michael Palin are both tales of family holidays coming unraveled, both based directly or indirectly on the respective writer's memories of their own seaside trips in the 1950s.

All Day On The Sands depicts the Cooper family's attempts to enjoy themselves on holiday at Morecambe, a choice of destination forced upon them by the father's lack of employment, and something of a come-down after the previous year's holiday in Minorca when the father was still in work. As with much of Bennett's work, *All Day On The Sands* is an exercise in the stressful maintenance of facades in the name of protecting a perceived social class standing. The Coopers, having fallen upon relatively hard times, are desperate to keep up appearances while on holiday, at all costs keeping the father's employment situation a secret from their fellow guests and hosts at their place of residence, the Miramar boarding house. The Miramar itself is a horrific artifice. The proprietor Mr Cattley intones proudly about the 'Riviera feel' that he has instigated as a means of competing with continental holiday experiences. Guests are invited to take breakfast in the 'Portofino Room' where they are subjected, via a public address system, to Cattley's florid, unctuous descriptions of the culinary delights that await them, whilst being reminded of the elaborate options available for their specially prepared packed lunches which can be collected from the 'Marbella Lounge'. The culinary contrivances are largely exploded by a crabby waitress with ill-fitting dentures who joylessly offers a choice of 'flakes or segments' as the guests' breakfast starter. When faced with the shallow disposability of her

Miramar-provided lunchbox contents, Mrs. Cooper protests "All this plastic cutlery. Little salt and pepper. It's pretend we're on an aeroplane...it's all splother. All of a sudden everything has to be a performance." An ironic outburst considering the levels of performance the character is prepared to reach herself in order to keep her husband's unemployment a secret.

Michael Palin's *East Of Ipswich* follows the exploits of the Burrill family, in particular son Richard, as they set about the arduous task of enjoying themselves on holiday at the East Anglian resort of Southwold. Palin mined his own pent-up teenage experiences of tedious family holidays in the late 1950s spent in drab coastal resorts when writing *East of Ipswich*. There is the gargoyle of a landlady who runs her B&B like a seaside stalag, the gruesome couple whom his parents invariably befriend, and ultimately there is an escape from the tedium through the lascivious young holidaymaker who drags Richard away from his parents and into a world of adolescent fumblings among the dunes. *East Of Ipswich* shares numerous ingredients with *All Day On The Sands*. For example the Burrills like the Coopers expend much energy in maintaining a veneer of respectability when in the presence of fellow guests. When asked, Mr. Burrill indicates that his profession is "light engineering" which earlier events would suggest amounts to designing hand driers for public conveniences. After running the guest house breakfast gauntlet there is also the inevitable daily ritual of the short walk to the beach and the family's stilted attempts to enjoy themselves. However it is the illicit satisfaction of young Richard's carnal needs that define the film. In the car en route to Southworld we catch an early glimpse of his frustrations:

RICHARD: "I mean, what is there east of Ipswich?"

MR BURRILL: "Only some of the most unspoilt and beautiful coastal scenery in the country"

RICHARD: "I want to go somewhere spoilt"

There is every reason to believe that television writers will continue to draw on the unique "somewhere spoilt" qualities provided by the English seaside. Recent series such as *Blackpool* (BBC, 2004) through its Dennis Potter-esque song-miming punctuations and *Funland* (BBC, 2005) through its Twin Peaks-styled blend of dark edged mystery with surreal humour and gritty drama have certainly added a post-modern twist on proceedings, in part picking up on the latter-day celebration of seaside resorts as quirky anachronistic treasures.

Bibliography

Anderson, Lindsay, Ryan, Paul (ed.): *Never Apologise: The Collected Writings of Lindsay Anderson*. London : Plexus 2004

Arnott, Jake: Mad, bad and dangerous to know. *The Guardian* Saturday 20 July 2002 p.31

Bakhtin, Mikhail Mikhaĭlovich: *Rabelais and his world*; translated by Helene Iswolsky. Cambridge, Mass. ; London : MIT Press 1968

Bakhtin, Mikhail Mikhaĭlovich: *Problems of Dostoevsky's poetics*; edited and translated by Caryl Emerson ; introduction by Wayne C. Booth. Manchester : Manchester University Press 1984

Balcon, Michael: *A lifetime of films*. London : Hutchinson 1969

Barton, Susan: *Working-class organisations and popular tourism, 1840-1970*. Manchester : Manchester University Press 2005

Baudrillard, Jean. Simulacra and Simulation.. Tr. Sheila Faria Glaser. Ann Arbor: University of Michigan. 1994.

Bennett, Tony: 'Hegemony, ideology, pleasure: Blackpool', in Bennett, Tony et al (eds.) *Popular Culture and Social Relations*, Milton Keynes : Open University Press 1986

Bracewell, Michael: The last resort. *The Independent on Sunday* 22 February 2004 p.37

Braggs, Steven and Harris, Diane: *Sun, fun and crowds: seaside holidays between the wars*. Stroud : Tempus 2000

Burchill, Julie: Brighton rocks. *The Guardian* Friday 25 July 2003 p.24

Burton, Alan: Death or glory? The Great War in British film. In Monk, Claire and Sargeant, Amy (eds.): *British Historical Cinema : the history, heritage, and costume film*. London : Routledge 2002 pp. 31-46

Cohen, Stanley: *Folk Devils and Moral Panics*. London : MacGibbon and Kee 1972

Dunne, Gillian A., Prendergast, Shirley, Telford David: Young, gay, homeless and invisible: a growing population? *Culture, Health & Sexuality* v. 4 n.1 2002 pp.103-115

Evans, Gareth: Andrew Kötting – profile. *Luxonline* http://www.luxonline.org.uk/articles/essays/andrew_kotting/detail5.html [consulted on 27.05.2006]

Evans, Peter William: *Carol Reed*. Manchester : Manchester University Press 2005

Fox, Kate: *Watching the English: the hidden rules of English behaviour*. London : Hodder & Stoughton 2004

Geddes, Andrew P.: *The Politics of Migration and Immigration in Europe.* London : Sage 2003

Greene, Graham: *Brighton rock*. Harmondsworth : Penguin Books 1970

Hare, William: *Early Film Noir: greed, lust and murder Hollywood style*. London : McFarland 2003

Holden, Anthony: *Olivier*. London : Weidenfeld and Nicolson 1988

Isaak, Jo Anna: *Feminism and contemporary art: The revolutionary power of women's laughter*. London : Routledge 1996

Kirkham, Nicola: Candy-coated chronotope: spatial representations of a seaside resort. In Miles, Malcolm and Kirkham, Nicola (eds.): *Cultures and settlements: advances in art and urban futures vol.3.* Bristol : Intellect Books 2003 pp.69-74

Lambert, Gavin: Free Cinema. *Sight and Sound* Spring 1956 pp.173-177

Lay, Samantha: Good intentions, high hopes and low budgets: Contemporary social realist film-making in Britain. *New Cinemas: Journal of Contemporary Film* v.5 n.3 2007 pp. 231-244

Mallan, Kerry, Pearce, Sharyn (eds.): *Youth cultures: texts, images and identities*. Westport, CT : Praeger 2003

Marriott, Stephanie: Dialect and dialectics in a British war film. *Journal of Sociolinguistics* v.1 n.2 1997 pp.173-193

Martin, Adrian: *Phantasms: the dreams and desires at the heart of our popular culture*. Harmondsworth : Penguin 1994

Medhurst, Andy: Unhinged invention. *Sight and Sound* v.5 n.10 October 1995 pp.6-10

Rabinowitz, Mark: Mark Herman sings out on "Little Voice". *IndieWIRE: People* http://www.indiewire.com/people/int_Herman_Mark_981214.html [consulted on 27.5.2006]

Richards, Jeffrey: 'Cul-de-sac England': The Ladykillers, in Richards, Jeffrey and Aldgate, Anthony (eds.): *Best of British :cinema and society from 1930 to the present*. London : Tauris 1999 pp.149-166

Richardson, Tony: *The long distance runner: a memoir.* London : Faber and Faber 1993

Shields, Rob: *Places on the margin: alternative geographies of modernity.* London : Routledge 1991

Shotter, John: *The cultural politics of everyday life: social constructionism, rhetoric and knowledge of the third kind.* Buckingham: Open University Press, 1993

Sinclair, Ian: Big Granny and Little Eden. *Sight and Sound* v.7 n.9 September 1997 pp.18-21

The Punch and Judy Man: Interview with Tony Hancock. *Films and Filming* v.8 n.11 August 1962 p.9

Todman, Dan: The reception of the Great War in the 1960s. *Historical Journal of Film, Radio and Television* v. 22, n. 1 2002 pp.29-36

Urbain, Jean-Didier: *At the beach*; translated by Catherine Porter. Minneapolis, Minn. ; London : University of Minnesota Press 2003

Urry, John: *The tourist gaze.* London : Sage 2001

Walton, John K.: *The British seaside: holidays and resorts in the twentieth century.* Manchester : Manchester University Press 2000

Walton, John K.: 'Respectability takes a holiday: disreputable behaviour at the Victorian seaside, in Hewitt, Martin (ed.) *Unrespectable recreations.* Leeds: Leeds Centre for Victorian Studies 2001

Warnes, Anthony et al: *Homelessness Factfile.* Sheffield Institute for Studies on Ageing, University of Sheffield. London : Crisis 2003

Waugh, Auberon: The Candy-coated mountain. *The Guardian* Saturday 25 August 1979 p.15

Webb, Darren: Bakhtin at the seaside: Utopia, modernity and the Carnivalesque. *Theory, Culture & Society* v. 22 n.3 2005 pp.121–138

Filmography

Primary texts:

A Visit to the Seaside (George Arthur Smith 1908)
Hindle Wakes (Maurice Elvey 1926)
Bank Holiday (Carol Reed 1938)
Brighton Rock (John Boulting 1947)
Holiday Camp (Ken Annakin 1947)
O Dreamland (Lindsay Anderson 1953)
Barnacle Bill (Charles Frend 1957)
The Entertainer (Tony Richardson 1960)
The Punch and Judy Man (Jeremy Summers 1963)
The System (Michael Winner 1964)
Oh! What a Lovely War (Richard Attenborough 1969)
All Day On The Sands (Giles Foster 1979)
Quadrophenia (Franc Roddam 1979)
Mona Lisa (Neil Jordan 1986)
East Of Ipswich (Tristram Powell 1987)
The Fruit Machine (Phillip Saville 1988)
Bhaji On The Beach (Gurinder Chadha 1993)
Funny Bones (Peter Chelsom 1995)
Gallivant (Andrew Kötting 1998)
I Want You (Michael Winterbottom 1998)
Little Voice (Mark Herman 1998)
Last Resort (Pawel Pawlikowski 2000)
GYPO (Jan Dunn 2005)
Ghosts (Nick Broomfield 2006)
London To Brighton (Paul Andrew Williams 2006)

Secondary texts:

The Brighton Strangler (Max Nosseck 1945)
Pink String And Sealing Wax (Robert Hamer 1946)
Good Time Girl (David MacDonald 1948)
Last Holiday (Henry Cass 1950)
Green Grow The Rushes (Derek N. Twist 1951)
Penny points To Paradise (Tony Young 1951)
Genevieve (Henry Cornelius 1953)
The Girl On The Pier (Lance Comfort 1953)
The Green Man (Robert Day 1956)
Jigsaw (Val Guest 1962)
Shadow of Fear (Ernest Morris 1963)
The Beauty Jungle (Val Guest 1964)
Crooks In Cloisters (Jeremy Summers 1964)
Smokescreen (Jim O'Connolly 1964)
Be My Guest (Lance Comfort 1965)
Every Day's A Holiday (James Hill 1965)
Cul-De-Sac (Roman Polanski 1966)
The Birthday Party (William Friedkin 1968)
Get Carter (Mike Hodges 1971)
The Flesh And Blood Show (Pete Walker 1972)
Carry On Girls (Gerald Thomas 1973)
Confessions From A Holiday Camp (Norman Cohen 1977)
The Supergrass (Peter Richardson 1985)
Wish You Were Here (David Leland 1987)
The Witches (Nicholas Roeg 1990)
Dirty Weekend (Michael Winner 1993)
Smart Alek (Andrew Kötting 1993)
Blue Juice (Carl Prechezer 1995)
Intimate Relations (Phillip Goodhew 1996)
The End Of The Affair (Neil Jordan 1999)

The War Zone (Tim Roth 1999)
Circus (Rob Walker 2000)
The Baby Juice Express (Michael Hurst 2001)
Last Orders (Fred Schepisi 2001)
The Lawless Heart (Tom Hunsinger / Neil Hunter 2001)
The Martins (Tony Grounds 2001)
Ashes And Sand (Bob Blagden 2002)
Heartlands (Damien O'Donnell 2002)
Blackball (Mel Smith 2003)
The Margate Exodus (Penny Woolcock 2007)

Index of people, places and films

All Day On The Sands 54
Anderson, Lindsay 17, 18, 19, 26, 44
Annakin, Ken 12, 14, 17
Attenborough, Richard 48, 49

Bakhtin, Mikhail 6, 15, 21
Bank Holiday 12-14, 15, 17, 24
Barnacle Bill 44-45, 47
Baudrillard, Jean 3
Bed-Sitting Room, The 49
Bennett, Alan 54
Benny Hill Show, The 54
Betjeman, John 51
Bexhill-on-Sea 51
Bhaji On The Beach 22-24, 26
Blackpool 9, 10, 11, 22-23, 26, 45, 50
Blackpool 55
Bognor Regis 47
Boulting, John 33
Bournemouth 47
Brassed Off 40
Brighton 2, 12, 20-21, 31-32, 33, 35, 37, 39, 48, 49
Brighton Rock 33-35, 36
Bristol 32
Broomfield, Nick 29, 30
Butlin, Billy 9, 14, 15, 16
By The Sea 54

Cartwright, Jim 40
Cattaneo, Peter 40
Chadha, Gurinder 22, 23, 26
Chelsom, Peter 50
Cleethorpes 51
Cornelius, Henry 44
Crichton, Charles 44
Croft, David 54

Davidson, Harold 9
Dean, Basil 15
Dover 21, 27
Dunn, Jan 29

East Of Ipswich 54-55
Eisenstein, Sergei 10
Elvey, Maurice 10, 11
Entertainer, The 45-46
Fawlty Towers 54
Filey 14, 16
Frend, Charles 44
Fruit Machine, The 31-33
Full Monty, The 40
Funland 55
Funny Bones 50, 51

Gallivant 51-52
Genevieve 44

Ghosts 29-31
Great Yarmouth 2
Greene, Graham 33
Griffith, D.W. 10
Guinness, Alec 44
GYPO 29-30

Hancock, Tony 47
Hastings 35
Herman, Mark 40
Hi-De-Hi 54
Hindle Wakes 9-11, 13, 18
Holiday Camp 12, 14-17, 45
How I Won The War 49
Hunstanton 44

I Want You 35-37, 38
Ibsen, Henrik 9

Jordan, Neil 37, 38

King & Country 49
Knight, Esmond 16
Kötting, Andrew 51-52

Last Resort 26-29, 30, 31, 33, 38
Lester, Richard 49
Little Voice 40-41
Littlewood, Joan 48, 49
Lockwood, Margaret 13, 14, 24
London To Brighton 38-40
Losey, Joseph 49

McGill, Donald 3, 54
Mackendrick, Alexander 44
Maggie, The 44
Margate 2, 17, 18, 26, 29, 30, 44
Minorca 54
Mona Lisa 37-38
Morecambe 30, 45, 54

O Dreamland 17-18, 19, 22, 44
Olivier, Laurence 46
Osborne, John 45

Palin, Michael 54, 55
Passport to Pimlico 44, 45
Pawlikowski, Pawel 26, 28, 29, 30
Perry, Jimmy 54
Potter, Dennis 55
Price, Dennis 15
Punch and Judy Man, The 46-48

Quadrophenia 20-21

Reed, Carol 12-14
Reed, Oliver 19
Richardson, Tony 45
Robson, Flora 15
Roddam, Franc 20

Saville, Phillip 31
Scarborough 40
Sing As We Go 15
Skegness 9
Smith, George Arthur 2

Southwold 55
Summers, Jeremy 46
System, The 19-20, 21, 28, 33

Titfield Thunderbolt, The 44
Torquay 54
Turner, Victor 6, 7, 24
Two Ronnies, The 54

Visit to the Seaside, A 2

Wadsworth, Edward 3
Williams, Paul Andrew 38
Willis, Ted 15
Winner, Michael 19
Winterbottom, Michael 35

www.ingramcontent.com/pod-product-compliance
Ingram Content Group UK Ltd.
Pitfield, Milton Keynes, MK11 3LW, UK
UKHW021322180426
11947UKWH00015B/1378